W9-AHO-108

Faces *from the* Past

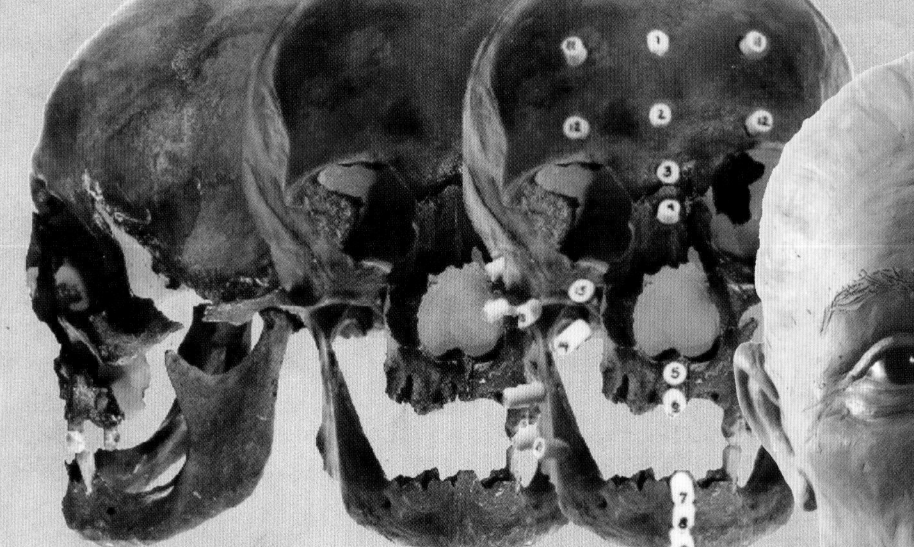

Pearl from Colonial Albany

Faces *from the* Past

FORGOTTEN PEOPLE OF NORTH AMERICA

by James M. Deem

Houghton Mifflin Books for Children
Houghton Mifflin Harcourt
Boston New York

For three incredible artists:

AMANDA DANNING, SHARON LONG, GAY MALIN

Houghton Mifflin Books for Children is an imprint of Houghton Mifflin Harcourt Publishing Company.

www.hmhbooks.com

Book design by YAY! Design.
The text of this book is set in Warnock Pro.

Illustration credits can be found on page 152.
Maps by YAY! Design.

Library of Congress Cataloging-in-Publication Data

Deem, James M.
Faces from the past : forgotten people of North America / by James M. Deem.
p. cm.
ISBN 978-0-547-37024-8
1. Forensic anthropology—North America. 2. Human remains (Archaeology)—North America. 3. Radiocarbon dating—North America. 4. Facial reconstruction (Anthropology)—North America. I. Title.
GN69.8.D44 2012
599.9—dc23
3117 2012006819

Manufactured in China
SCP 10 9 8 7 6 5 4 3
4500456928

Contents

Introduction

Once, no humans lived on the continent of North America; then they began to journey here.

The first migrants arrived perhaps fifteen or twenty thousand years ago. Scientists believe that people from Asia had settled on a one-thousand-mile-wide land bridge (now called Beringia) that connected present-day Siberia to Alaska. Eventually, some of their descendants moved onward to North America and spread out across the land.

Much later, others came—from Europe, from Africa, from Asia and other places. Some came willingly; some were enslaved and brought against their will.

But all settled on this continent.

And when the earliest settlers of North America died, so long ago, they were buried in caves or isolated graves. Later, others built burial mounds or cemeteries for their dead. Over time, many of the mounds were robbed and destroyed. Many early cemeteries disappeared from sight when makeshift grave markers blew away in the wind or decayed. Sometimes the early dead were not even buried; they simply fell where they were wounded and came to rest where they lay. No matter how they died or were buried, as time passed these people were forgotten.

Today, when skeletons from centuries ago are discovered, scientists want to study them to discover information about the lives and deaths of these people, about their time and place in history. Sometimes artists are asked to reconstruct faces from the past, using replicas of their skulls. Then these nameless, unknown people can be brought back to life, remembered, and honored.

Now, when their skeletons are discovered, their stories can be told.

In the 1940s, Sidney and Georgia Wheeler explored caves in the rocky ridges that rose from the desert flats of central and northern Nevada.

CHAPTER 1

THE MAN *from Spirit Cave*

The man was very ill on the last day of his life. His people fed him, near the edge of the marsh where they lived. When he died, they carried him up a slope to a shallow cave. There they dug his grave, lined it with sagebrush, and placed his wrapped body inside before covering it with dirt. No one suspected that his final rest would be disturbed many thousands of years later.

Georgia and Sidney Wheeler had heard all about the mysterious cave.

As archaeologists working for the Nevada State Parks Commission in 1940, the husband-and-wife team had been told many times about a cave with a "blocked-up" area in the back. The only trouble was that no one could remember exactly where it was.

Because their job was to identify caves that were once used by prehistoric people and salvage any artifacts found inside before they were destroyed or stolen, they figured they would run across the cave one day. They had a lot of territory to cover, trying to rescue the caves from two particular groups of people: bat-guano miners and pot hunters. The miners, unaware of the caves' historic importance, collected bat excrement, called guano, and sold it for fertilizer, but in removing the guano, they often carelessly destroyed the items left behind by early people. The pot hunters, however, knew that many Nevada caves contained valuable Native American artifacts that they could sell or keep for their own illegal collections.

Ten thousand years ago Lake Lahontan covered vast stretches of what has become present-day Nevada.

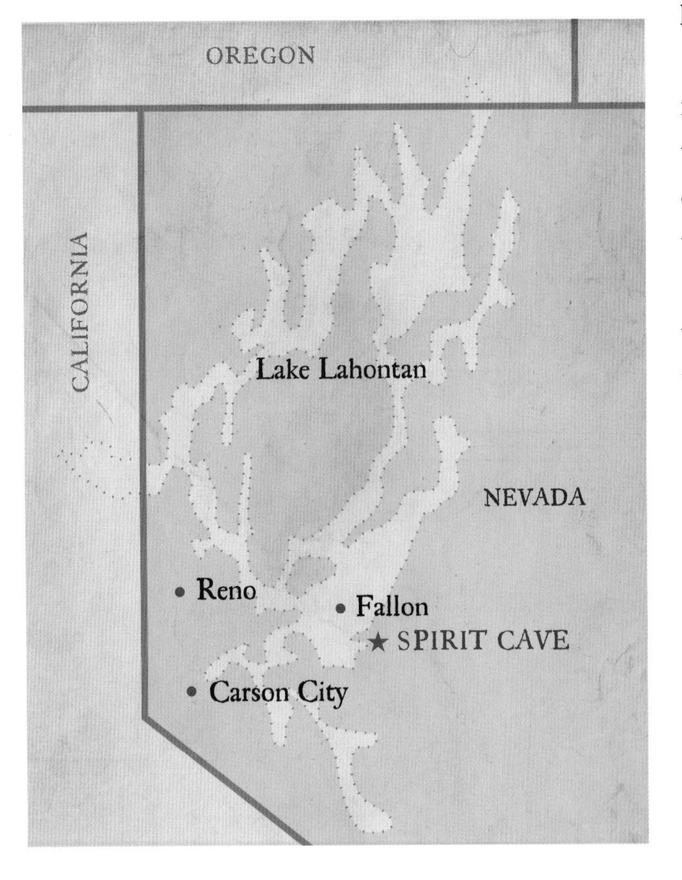

During the day, the Wheelers drove through isolated areas looking for caves to investigate before they were ransacked. At night they often camped out far from civilization, sleeping in the back of their station wagon.

One August evening after dinner, the Wheelers were sitting in their camp discussing the caves that they needed to visit when the subject of the mysterious "blocked-up" cave arose. They had noticed a small cave in the rocky outcrop above their camp and wondered whether it might fit the description. They decided to find out before sunset.

Sidney led the way and had no sooner begun to climb the slope than he heard the warning sound of a rattlesnake. Although he couldn't see the rattler, he believed it was in front of him. Quickly, instinctively, he stepped backwards without looking and stumbled over a large rock, injuring his leg.

The early people of the area lived on the shore of Lake Lahontan. Only remnants of the lake remain now, including the Stillwater Marsh, near Fallon, Nevada.

For the next few days his leg was in such pain that he could not kneel, and so the Wheelers changed their plans. Instead of exploring caves, they stopped climbing and simply walked across the desert, scouting for caves that they might have missed. They hoped Sidney's leg would heal faster that way. On one of those unplanned days, the couple chose to investigate Spirit Cave, a small site they had noticed many times and dismissed. That day, August 11, 1940, would turn out to be an important one in North American archaeology, though no one would know it for more than fifty years.

The Wheelers walked a mile over the desert flats that more than thirteen thousand years ago had formed the bed of an enormous lake (now called Lake Lahontan). Some of the descendants of the earliest people who came to North America lived on the marshy shores of the lake, which was bordered by rocky terraces. Over time, waves had

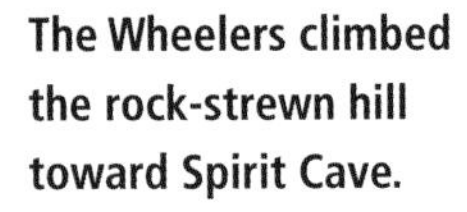

The Wheelers climbed the rock-strewn hill toward Spirit Cave.

carved shallow caves, called rock shelters, into the rocks. The early people who lived there used the caves for storage, shelter, and sometimes burial. Eventually, Lake Lahontan dried up, leaving the sandy desert flats lined with cave-filled ridges that would one day reveal information about the early people of the region . . . if guano miners and pot hunters didn't destroy them first.

After they reached the opening of Spirit Cave that day, the Wheelers were tired from their hike. They rested and surveyed the entrance. They saw immediately that Spirit Cave did not snake its way deep underground. Instead, it was a shallow, rocky overhang with one small cave chamber and nothing more. Sidney was so disappointed that once he had made his initial inspection, he announced that he was ready to leave.

But, as he wrote in his field notes, Georgia wanted to excavate a small area to see if the cave contained any signs of prehistoric humans. "[She] insisted that I select the location. Finally, to keep her quiet, I pointed at random to a slightly raised portion of the floor which was bordered by a scattered line of rocks and she began to dig. The first foot revealed no evidence of occupation, just dry, dusty, wind-blown sand filling the spaces between the rocks. The next sweep of her trowel laid bare a small section of a large mat . . . of split tule."

The mat was woven from tule (or bulrushes), a type of reed that once grew along the lakeshore outside the cave. Georgia removed the rest of the sand from the top of the

At first, Spirit Cave looked like an unimpressive rock shelter to Sidney Wheeler. Its opening is barely visible beneath the rocky overhang.

mat and gently opened it. Inside were a few human bones, the remains of an ancient person who had been buried there.

As Georgia enlarged the excavation pit so that she could remove the burial without damage, she discovered a second well-preserved mat beneath it. Intrigued, Sidney forgot about his injured leg and joined his wife to help with the excavation. The couple quickly learned that this mat held another, larger burial.

If he had known how important the second burial was to become, perhaps Sidney would have written more in his field notes. As it was, so much of what happened during the next few weeks is unrecorded, except for minimal details.

"After much tedious work and a trip to [Fallon, Nevada] to secure assistance," Sidney wrote, "we took the necessary photographs and transferred the complete burial intact to a stretcher which was placed on our bed in the station wagon." What he didn't mention was how many people assisted them or even how long it took. Without considerable help, they would not have been able to lift the fragile remains, place the mat-wrapped body on a stretcher, and carry it over a mile to their station wagon. They drove back to Fallon with the body to the office of a local doctor named Sawyer.

There they carefully examined the burial, starting with the wrappings. Three mats encased the body. The outer one, a large thirty-five-by-fifty-inch "sleeping mat" made mostly of tule, was tied under the feet. It was rough and coarse, but the two inner

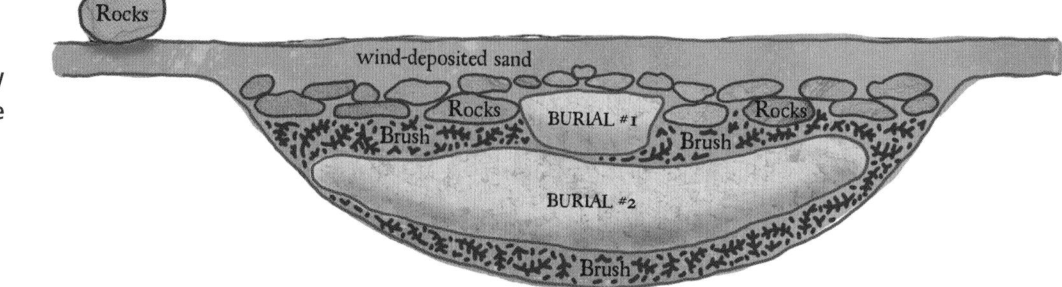

Sidney Wheeler sketched a diagram of the Spirit Cave burials (recreated by an artist here) to file with his field notes of the discovery.

mats—one sewn together at the head that covered the top half of the body, the other wrapped around the bottom half—were much softer and more flexible. Finely woven with a diamond-plaited technique and then sewn together, they were made from cattails and tule.

Then they opened the matting and saw the body of a man. He was curled in a fetal position, lying on his right side atop a blanket or robe made from rabbit skin. Each skin, it was later learned, was cut into one long, thin piece (the way an apple might be peeled in one strip) and then woven together to form the blanket. He wore a pair of patched moccasins made from three types of animal hide and lined with woven pieces of tule

This photograph of Spirit Cave, taken in 2011, shows the general location where the burials were unearthed: behind the large area of rocks in the center.

Sidney Wheeler photographed the body after it was removed from the burial pit. Georgia Wheeler's foot, leg, and hand are visible in the back right of the photo, along with the trowel that she used in the excavation.

that served as socks. The bottom half of his body had become a skeleton, but the upper part was partially mummified. The dry rock shelter—and the layers of matting and rabbit-skin robe—had helped preserve some of his skin; it was like very dry leather. His head had even retained its scalp and some shoulder-length tufts of hair.

For nine days the Wheelers kept the body in the back of their car while they excavated the rest of the cave, sleeping elsewhere at night. On the tenth day they were able to take the body to the Parks Commission in Carson City. Soon afterward, the body was examined by the archaeologist Mark Harrington, who had trained the Wheelers. Harrington estimated that the man had died between fifteen hundred and two thousand years earlier. Then, on August 30 and 31, less than two weeks after the discovery, the man's body was exhibited at the Nevada State Fair in Reno, where he was identified as "Oscar, a partially mummified Indian skeleton."

After that, the body was placed in a wooden box, covered with mothballs, and

When the body of Spirit Cave Man was unwrapped, the Wheelers saw a partially preserved man, as shown in this drawing by the artist Sharon Long.

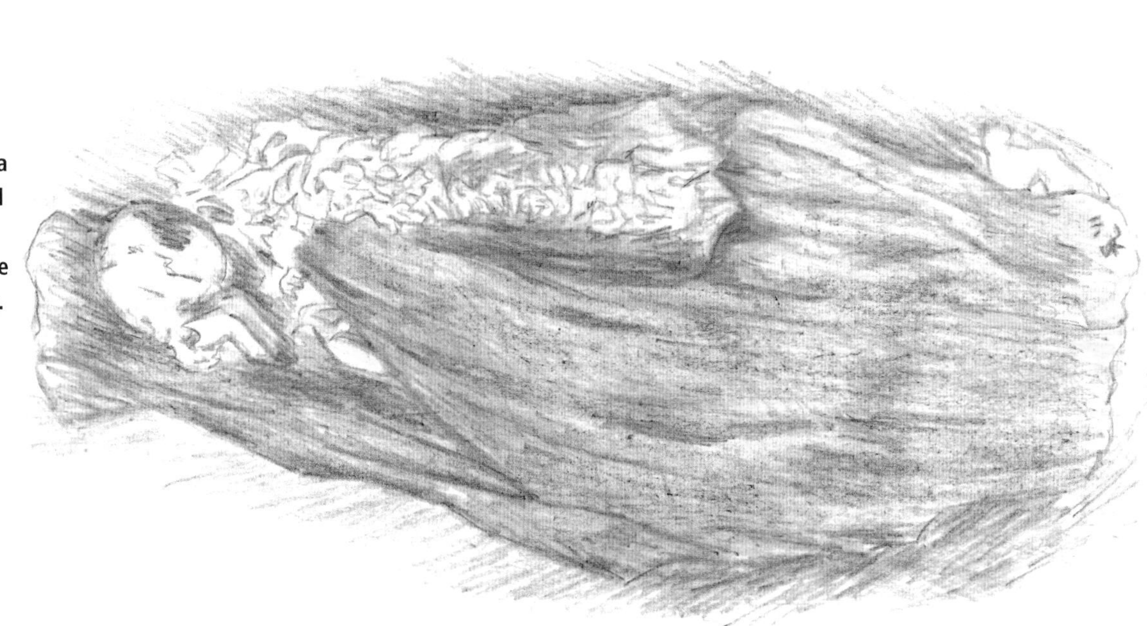

Archaeologists and Anthropologists

The Wheelers were archaeologists; Ervin Taylor was an anthropologist. But what do those two terms mean?

Anthropologists are scientists who study human behavior (cultural anthropology), language (linguistic anthropology), human development (physical or biological anthropology), and past cultures (archaeology). *Archaeologists* are anthropologists who specialize in excavating and recovering items from historic sites, analyzing them, and interpreting their meaning. If an archaeologist studies human or animal remains found in archaeological sites, she is often called a *bioarchaeologist*, a relatively new term.

stored along with some eight hundred Native American remains taken from other Nevada caves, rock shelters, and burial sites. No one thought that it was the least bit important or noteworthy.

For fifty-four years, the man, now called Spirit Cave Man, lay undisturbed as the world of science went through many technological advances. In 1994, Ervin Taylor, a California anthropologist, wanted to improve upon the technique of radiocarbon dating human bones from ancient burials. He asked officials at the Nevada State Museum for samples of both bone and hair from any prehistoric human burials in the museum's collection. The museum provided Taylor samples from Spirit

Cave Man, who had been housed there since the museum's founding in 1941. When the initial radiocarbon dates proved to be so old that Taylor wondered if they were wrong, the museum sent samples from the mats that had surrounded the body for additional testing.

The final results confirmed Ervin's initial findings and stunned everyone involved. Spirit Cave Man had died not 1,500 or even 2,000 years ago. No, he had died approximately 10,500 years earlier, making his the oldest partially mummified human remains ever recovered in North America.

Consequently, many scientists wanted to unravel the mystery of who he was, how he lived, what he ate, and how he died. There was so much renewed interest in the burial that even scientists from the Smithsonian Institution in Washington, D.C., wished to study the body.

During 1995 and 1996, Spirit Cave Man was examined again and again by different anthropologists. His bones told them that Spirit Cave Man was about forty-five years old and five feet, two inches tall when he died. He suffered from arthritis and chronic lower-back pain. He had two notable wounds. Two bones in his right hand had been broken at some point but had healed long before he died. The side of his skull behind his left eye had been fractured nearer the time of his death. Anthropologists interpreted this type of head wound as evidence that he had been struck by a rock or a blunt object during a physical attack. Although this blow was a serious injury, the wound was not fatal and was in the process of healing when he died.

What may have killed him, they concluded, were three badly abscessed teeth. These molars had worn down so much that the inner pulp chambers were exposed

Spirit Cave Man and Radiocarbon Dating

To discover how long ago Spirit Cave Man lived, bone, hair, and mat samples were analyzed for the amount of an isotope called carbon 14 (C14) present in them. Every living thing contains carbon 14; after death the level of C14 begins to diminish. Scientists have a formula to calculate the age of an object based on the amount of C14 it contains.

The radiocarbon study found that Spirit Cave Man had lived about 9,400 years BP (before the present), based on the dates from his bone and hair. Even the three mats that wrapped him were made at roughly the same time. But radiocarbon years do not equal calendar years, since C14 fluctuates from year to year. When the radiocarbon years were recalculated as calendar years, scientists estimated that Spirit Cave Man had lived about 10,500 years ago.

to the air and caused severe infections in his gums and jawbone, which most likely entered his bloodstream.

None of these findings, though, was surprising or unexpected. Then anthropologists took a closer look at his skull. Because his body was discovered in a Nevada cave near the Fallon Paiute-Shoshone Tribe reservation, many people initially assumed that he was of Native American ancestry. But when some scientists examined his skull features, they came to another conclusion: Spirit Cave Man, with his long and narrow skull, would have looked very different from a modern-day Native American.

To show how this ancient man would have appeared when he was alive, the Nevada State Museum hired the sculptor Sharon Long in 1998 to make a life-size reconstruction of his face. Long was well prepared to recreate the face of Spirit Cave Man. With degrees in sculpture and anthropology, she had a thorough knowledge of the anatomy of the human face, as well as the artistic skill to create a face using precise scientific measurements.

When she was contacted by the museum, she knew exactly what she needed first: a replica of Spirit Cave Man's fragile and irreplaceable skull. To accomplish this, museum officials transported Spirit Cave Man's body to a local hospital, where the head was given a CT scan, a series of x-rays that produces a cross-sectional view. The data from the CT scan was then sent to a laboratory, where a machine called a stereolithograph projected a laser image of the three-dimensional skull onto liquid plastic. As the laser beam moved across the liquid, it hardened into the shape of Spirit Cave Man's skull.

This plastic copy was too expensive to use, however, and Long needed extra copies: one to study as a reference while working and one on which to build the face. Consequently, Long made a mold of the plastic skull using liquid rubber latex. With this mold, she could make as many inexpensive plaster casts of Spirit Cave Man's skull as she needed.

His Last Meals

Scientists collected and analyzed the contents of Spirit Cave Man's intestines. These coprolites (or fossilized feces) were washed to remove dust, dried for forty-eight hours, then placed in glass beakers and covered with saline solution so that they would dissolve. After a week's time, the now liquid samples were passed through a screen. The solid material that the screen trapped was analyzed for food content, while the liquid was tested for pollen. The solid samples indicated that Spirit Cave Man had last eaten small fish (complete with their eyes and bones) most likely caught with baskets or nets in the shallow water of Lake Lahontan near Spirit Cave. Pollen collected in the liquid samples suggested that Spirit Cave Man died in late winter or spring.

The sculptor Sharon Long inspects the plastic replica made from the skull of Spirit Cave Man.

The ridges visible on the top of this replica of Spirit Cave Man's skull are a result of the computer-generated reproduction process but do not affect the reconstruction.

After the plaster skull was finished, Long was almost ready to begin the reconstruction. First, though, she had to determine the thickness of Spirit Cave Man's face and its underlying muscles and tissue so that she could build the face as accurately as possible. To do this, she had to apply measurements many scientists had compiled over the years that indicated the thickness of the human face at specific points. Fortunately, Long could open a book and choose an appropriate measurement table to use.

But it hadn't always been that way.

Sharon Long made a mold of the plastic replica of Spirit Cave Man's skull, then used it to make inexpensive plaster copies.

Johann Sebastian Bach was buried in an unmarked grave in the churchyard of St. Johannes Church in Leipzig, Germany. The church was depicted in this 1840 illustration by the German artist J. Richter.

CHAPTER 2

MAKING FACES
from the Past

When he began to lose his eyesight, he agreed to an operation. When that failed, he allowed another. The result was complete blindness, and he died soon afterward. He was buried in the cemetery of a local church, his grave unmarked. He became more famous after death, and when his body was discovered many years later during excavations in the churchyard, his skull was used to bring him back to life.

Two early facial reconstructions were done using skulls from Leipzig, Germany, and Auvernier, Switzerland.

When the first facial reconstructions were completed in the late 1800s, scientists had to supply their own measurements.

In 1894, for example, the opportunity arose to locate the body of the famous composer Johann Sebastian Bach, who had died in 1750. During the 1800s, many other respected German writers and composers such as Beethoven had been exhumed from their graves, their skeletons examined and reburied in elaborate monuments.

Although Bach had been buried in the cemetery of St. Johannes Church in Leipzig, his grave was unmarked. When officials announced that they were going to renovate and enlarge the church in 1894, many realized that they might be able to locate Bach's body and give it a

The Earliest Faces

Even in ancient times people tried putting faces onto the skulls of people who once lived. In 1953, archaeologists excavating a house in Jericho (on the West Bank of the Palestinian Territories) found a number of skulls under the floor; they had plaster faces with cowrie-shell eyes applied to them. Called "over-modeled skulls," these primitive works from about 7000 B.C. are among the earliest examples of facial reconstruction, though they were not intended to be accurate representations.

In the sixteenth and seventeenth centuries, many artists studied how the human body was constructed, especially the muscles and glands. By observing doctors perform dissections

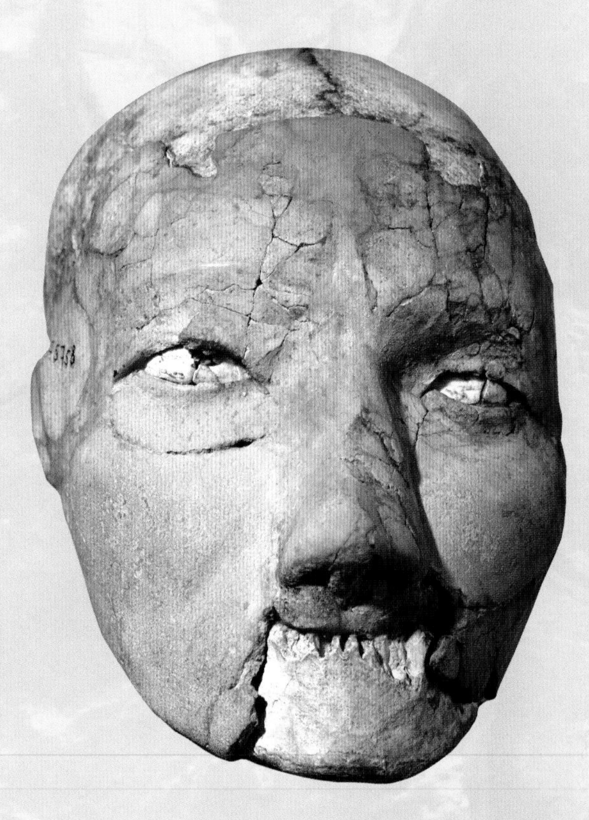

One of the earliest facial reconstructions done on a skull, the Jericho skull was not intended to be an accurate representation of the dead person.

more dignified final resting place, which his many admirers could visit.

With a little research, church officials discovered that Bach had been buried in an oak coffin in the churchyard, one of only twelve such coffins used in fourteen hundred burials during the year 1750. Local legend also said that he had been buried just six steps from the south door of the church. As workers excavated the area nearest the church, they were on the lookout for an oak coffin.

On October 22, 1894, around eleven in the morning, the workers found one. Church officials called the respected anatomist Wilhelm His to the churchyard in hopes that he could identify Bach's body. Although the coffin turned out to contain the skeleton of a young woman, workers soon found a second oak coffin. Inside, His saw the skeleton of an "elderly man, not very tall

Wilhelm His, a noted professor of anatomy in Leipzig, was asked by church officials to identify Bach's body. In order to verify the skeleton's identity, His decided to have the skull's face reconstructed.

and then drawing what was revealed, artists learned the underlying features and were able to educate others—gruesomely so. In some cases they made drawings and even wax models of a flayed body (that is, with its skin peeled back), revealing the various layers of tissue and muscles underneath to help train doctors. Their anatomically revealing faces have aided many artists who do facial reconstructions today.

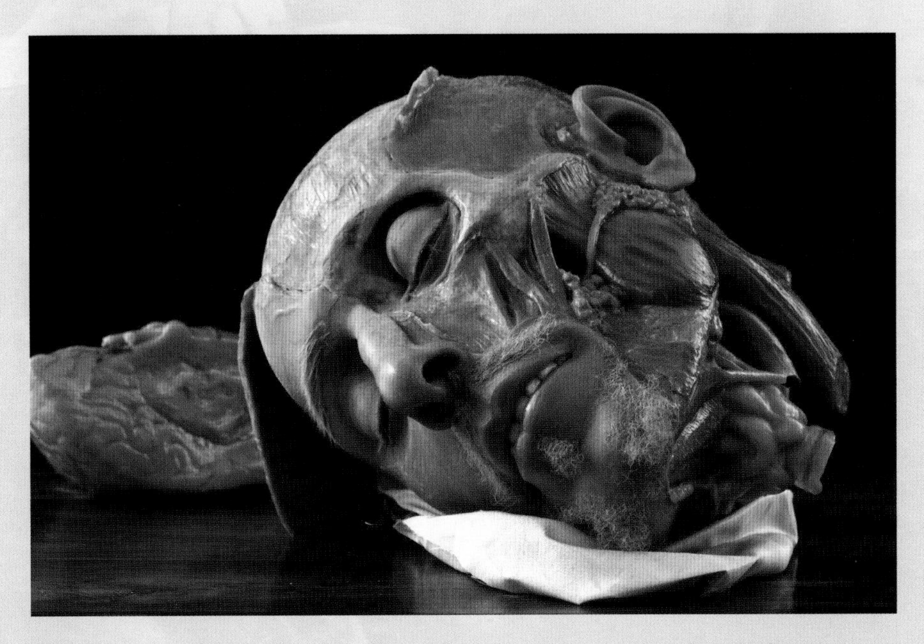

The Italian artist Gaetano Zumbo was the first person to create anatomical wax models, around 1700. Here is one of the first wax faces he created, the right half appearing normal, the left half revealing the facial muscles, blood vessels, and glands. He reconstructed the face on an actual skull rather than a replica. Today it is exhibited at La Specola museum in Florence, Italy.

but well-built," with a skull that was "sturdy and of strong features." His was certain that the remains belonged to a man of Bach's stature.

His took the skeleton back to his laboratory, where he laid out the bones and examined them. To verify that the skull was indeed Bach's, he compared it with two portraits painted of Bach during his lifetime. Although His believed that the comparison showed a clear similarity, he concluded that the only way to prove that the skull belonged to Bach was to make a plaster copy and build Bach's face out of clay upon it. This would be the one of the first facial reconstructions ever done.

As an anatomist, His realized that the success of a reconstruction depended on knowing the depth of the tissue on the human face. To determine this scientifically, he measured the faces of thirty-seven corpses he found in the local morgue. Nine had come from the penitentiary, where they had died of disease; their bodies were quite thin. The others had committed suicide, and their bodies were more substantial; among them

The artist Carl Seffner created a bust of Johann Sebastian Bach in 1895 to show that the skull found in the oak coffin had belonged to the famous composer.

Using a plaster copy of Bach's skull, Seffner demonstrated how he created the reconstruction of Bach's face, leaving half of the skull visible in one version of the bust.

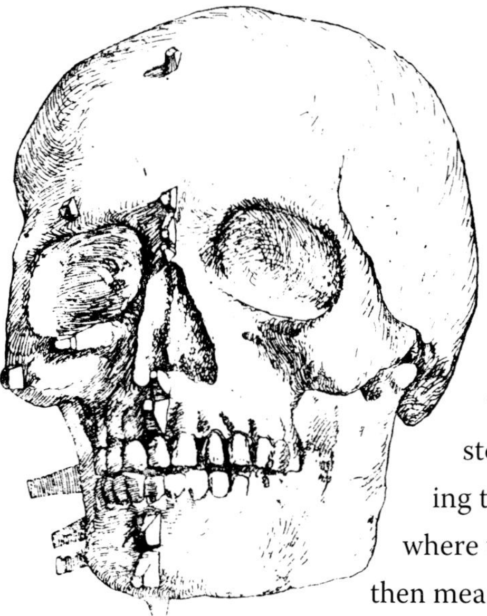

were eight older men. By inserting a sewing needle through a small piece of rubber and pressing the needle tip through the corpse's skin until it stopped at the skull, sliding the rubber to the point where the needle stopped, and then measuring the distance on the needle, His was able to calculate the tissue depth at fifteen specific locations on a human skull. The depth measurements for each location on the corpses were added together and then averaged. Then the fifteen depth measurements were given to an artist named Carl Seffner to guide him in the reconstruction of Bach's face.

His's experiment proved to be a success: Seffner's sculpture was favorably compared with portraits of Bach painted when he was alive. As a result, other anatomists and artists began to make facial reconstructions.

Next, the anatomist Julius Kollmann and the sculptor E. Buchly collaborated in 1898 on the facial reconstruction of an Iron Age woman whose ancient skull was found near Auvernier, Switzerland. To improve upon His's measurements, Kollmann measured twenty-eight more corpses and added three more measurement points on the skull for a total of eighteen. Kollmann also combined his measurements with those taken by His and averaged the numbers for each point. Instead of using a needle with sliding rubber, though, Kollmann used a soot-covered needle. When it was inserted into the skin, the needle was cleaned of soot; the clean area was then measured.

The sculptor E. Buchly created the face of an Iron Age woman (top and bottom) who lived in prehistoric times on the shores of Lake Neuchatel. The drawing of the skull (left) shows the placement of the tissue-depth markers.

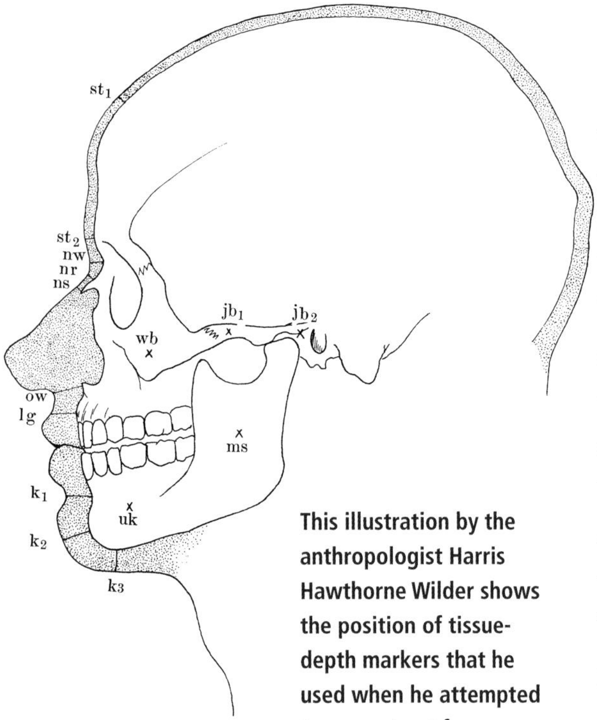

This illustration by the anthropologist Harris Hawthorne Wilder shows the position of tissue-depth markers that he used when he attempted to reconstruct faces on historic skulls in 1912.

Of course, there were drawbacks to the early reconstruction techniques. First, the skin and tissue of a dead person shrink and collapse, giving shallower depth measurements than would be found in a living person. What's more, anatomists could only measure the few bodies available in a morgue; they could not measure enough corpses at one time to develop reliable average tissue depths for men and women of all ages, body types, and ancestries. Over time, with technological advances, better tissue-depth tables were developed, giving measurements for thirty-two locations on the skull for all types of people. More recently, measurement tables have been developed by using ultrasound technology on living persons.

Early reconstructions were historical; the skulls of artistic geniuses and early people were turned into faces to help bring the past to life. Eventually, though, reconstructions began to be used in law enforcement, primarily to help police identify human remains. For example, a hiker might discover the skeleton of a person beside a forest path. Before the advent of DNA and other, more sophisticated technologies, police departments were often unable to identify such remains, especially if there were no missing-persons' reports. Artists would sometimes be called on to make a facial reconstruction in the hope that relatives or friends might be able to identify the person. The goal of the forensic (or criminal) artist was not to make an exact replica of the person's face when he was alive; rather, it was to make a close-enough match that a friend or relative would be able to identify the person. Even today police departments sometimes ask artists to reconstruct a face from a skull if it might aid in solving a difficult or important case.

To make certain that she used the appropriate tissue-depth tables for her reconstruction of Spirit Cave Man, Sharon Long consulted with Douglas Owsley, the head of the physical anthropology division at the Smithsonian Institution, who had also examined Spirit Cave Man. When she had selected her numbers, she cut each of the thirty-two rubber

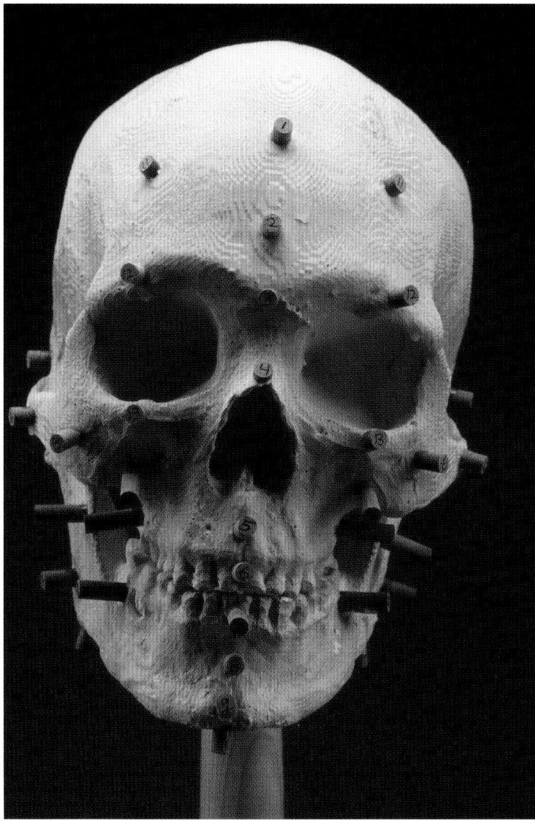

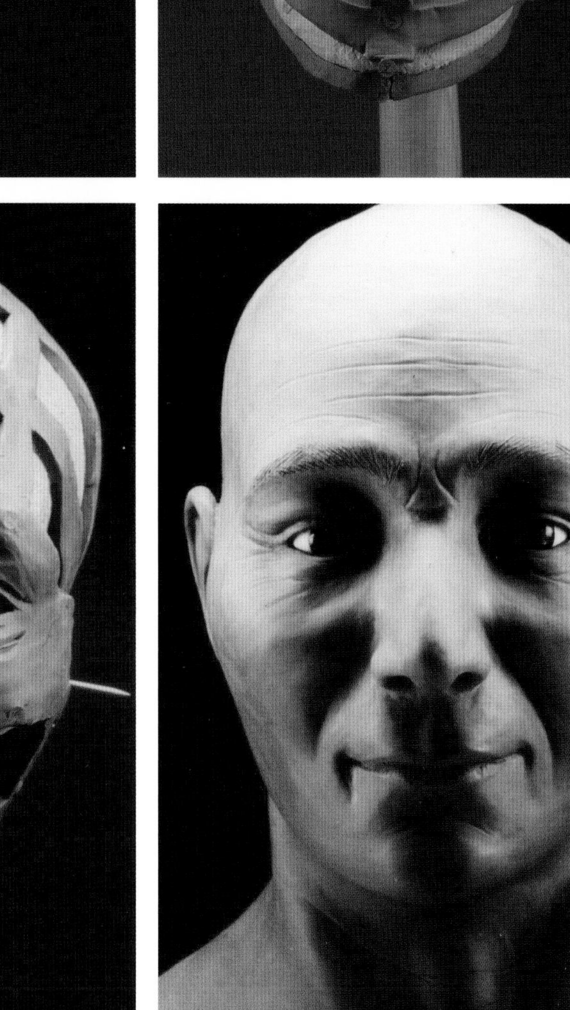

The artist Sharon Long built the face of Spirit Cave Man on a replica skull, making certain that she accurately positioned the tissue-depth markers at the correct length (top left), then gradually laid strips of clay onto the skull (top right, bottom left) to reconstruct the face. The final photograph (bottom right) shows the clay face before it was painted.

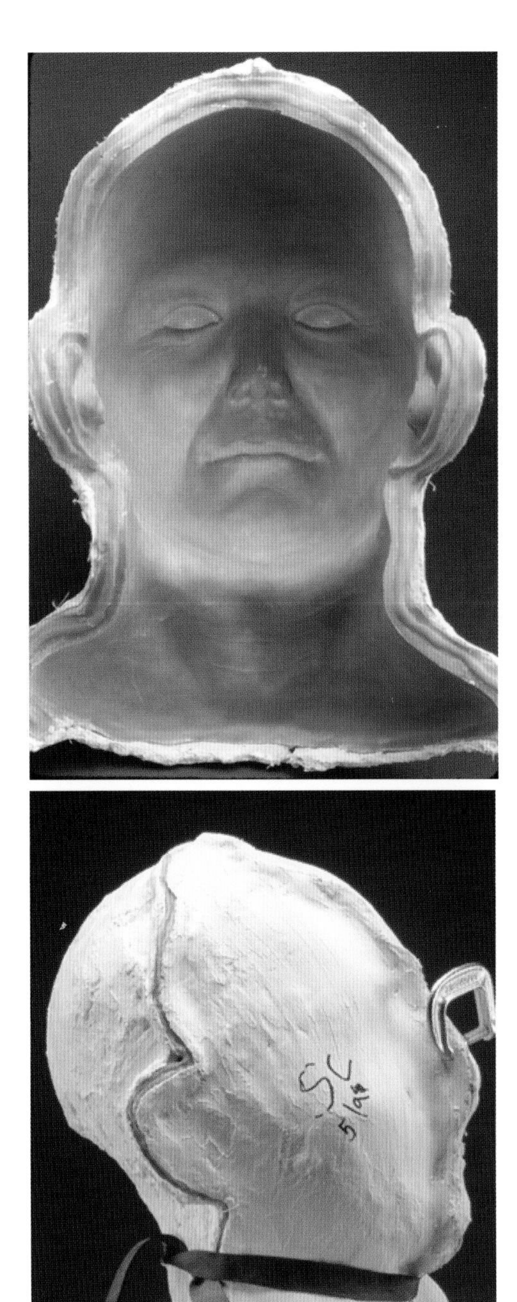

markers—much like pencil erasers—to the correct length and glued them in predetermined places on the replica skull. Ten markers went down the front of the skull; eleven were placed on each side. The markers indicated how thick the face should be at each location.

Next, Long laid strips of clay over the markers to the depth indicated. Then she built the nose and placed the glass eyes into their orbits. She carefully contoured his cheeks, chin, nose, mouth, eye sockets. She calculated how wide his mouth was by drawing a line down from each pupil to mark the end points of the mouth. She estimated the size of the ears by drawing lines from the bottom of the nose and the top of the eye sockets to each side of the face.

When she was finished sculpting the clay, she had one more face to make. Because the clay face would deteriorate over time, she had to make a mold of the finished face so that a permanent plaster cast could be made. The original clay face, however, would be destroyed in the process of making the mold.

Once Long had made the cast, she was able to apply color for the skin and paint on the finer details, such as the lips and the eyebrows. Although the tissue depth of a facial reconstruction is scientifically determined, other aspects depend on interpretation. These include the shape of the lips and ears; the position of the eyeballs inside the eye sockets; the manner in which the face shows age; the type of hairstyle; and the color of the eyes, hair, and skin, unless the person's scalp, hair, and even eyes were preserved, as they can be with mummified remains. Often the sculptor will consult with historians and scientists to make sure that the reconstruction is as authentic as possible.

When Sharon Long was finished, one of the oldest and best-preserved early North Americans had reawakened in the twenty-first century.

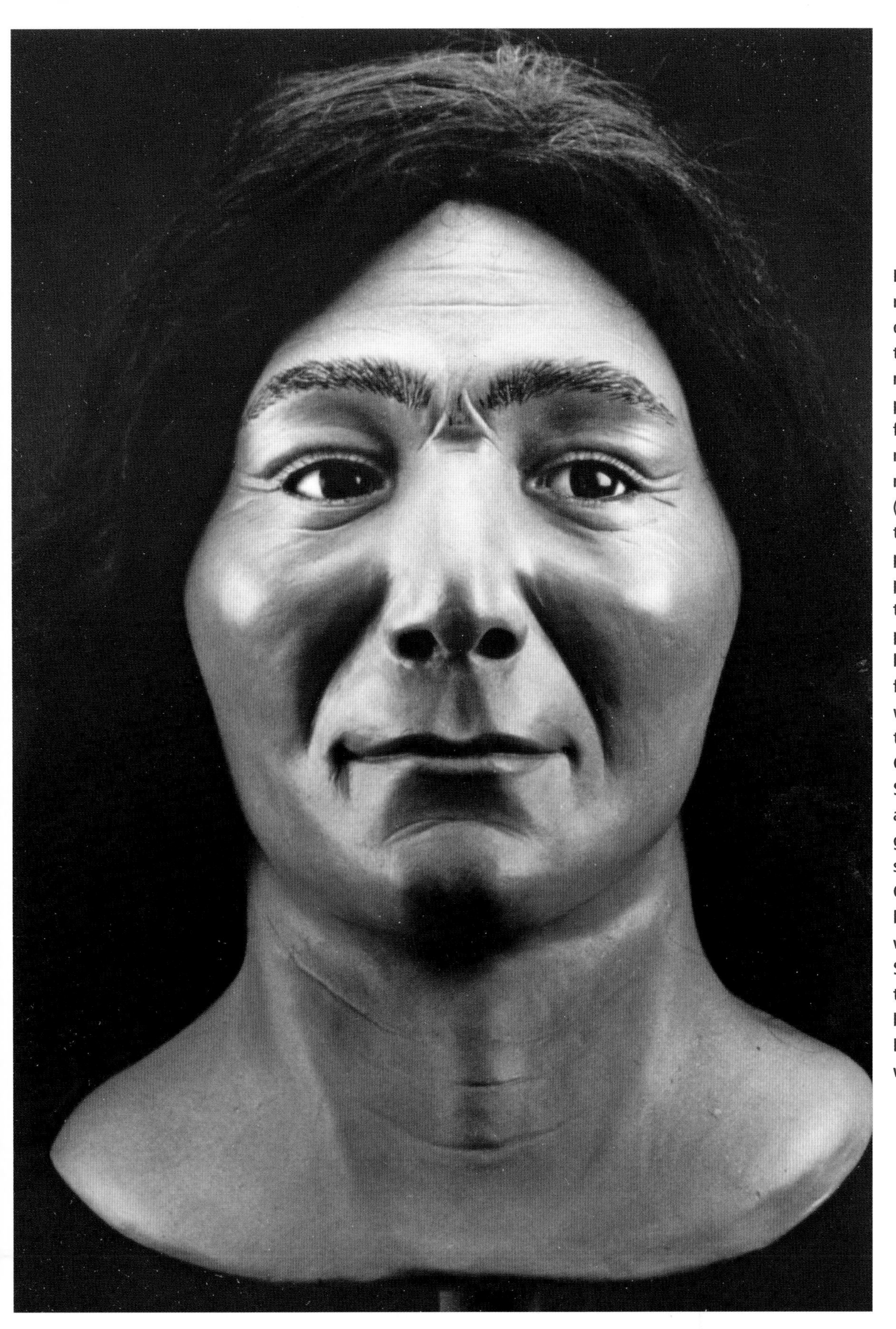

Because the clay reconstruction will deteriorate over time, the artist usually makes a permanent plaster cast of the face. First, Sharon Long made a two-part latex mold of the clay face (far left top). Because the latex would be too pliable when filled with plaster, she supported the mold with an outer plaster shell (far left bottom). Then she filled the double mold with plaster to create the final cast of Spirit Cave Man (near left). She painted the plaster and attached hair to give a more complete sense of what Spirit Cave Man would have looked like. Scientists who studied the hair of Spirit Cave Man noted that it would have been brown, shoulder-length, and somewhat wavy.

A Controversial Discovery: To Rebury or to Study?

Are the ancestors of Spirit Cave Man related to the Ainu of Japan (left) or to the Paiute of Nevada (right)? Without the permission of the Paiute-Shoshone Tribe, scientists are unable to conduct the DNA testing that would help determine Spirit Cave Man's genetic ancestors.

Because Spirit Cave Man was found on land belonging to the federal government, a special law passed in 1990 and called the Native American Graves Protection and Repatriation Act (NAGPRA) applied to his remains. According to NAGPRA, museums with human remains or artifacts affiliated with a Native American tribe were required to repatriate, or return, them to the tribe. In this case, the Fallon Paiute-Shoshone Tribe claimed

affiliation with Spirit Cave Man and asked for the return of his body. They believed that the man's spirit could not be at peace until his remains were reburied.

Anthropologists from the Nevada State Museum and other museums, however, claimed that Spirit Cave Man was unaffiliated with any Native American tribe. They based their belief, in part, on their analysis of Spirit Cave Man's skull. Some scientists concluded that his skull appeared to be more closely linked to the Ainu people of Japan; others wondered if it was closer to ancient people from Polynesia or Australia.

To find out more about Spirit Cave Man's ancestry, some scientists wanted to conduct DNA testing. This would clarify if Spirit Cave Man shared genetic ancestors with the Fallon Paiute-Shoshone Indians. If so, scientists would look for reasons that the skull shape had changed over time. If not, they would determine which people had similar genetic ancestors to Spirit Cave Man and whether his ancestors migrated from a different place from that of the ancestors of Native Americans.

DNA testing, however, required small samples from Spirit Cave Man that would be destroyed in the testing. The Paiute-Shoshone did not want his remains to be desecrated. To prevent further testing, the tribe filed a lawsuit claiming the man as an ancestor and requesting his return for reburial.

As of now, the fate of Spirit Cave Man is in limbo; he reportedly remains in storage at the Nevada State Museum awaiting a court decision on what will become of him. The facial reconstruction sculpted by Sharon Long is in storage as well; it was never exhibited because of the controversy.

Students Amelia Henry, Megan Thompson, and Josh Kirk of the Fernley Intermediate School in Nevada attempt to make their own facial reconstruction on a model of a human skull. Each year the students in Vivian Olds's class research the ancient man.

Plaster copies of some of the skulls found in the HRR at the University of Wyoming are used as teaching tools for anthropology students.

FORGOTTEN PEOPLE *of North America*

The man from Spirit Cave was neither the first nor the last historical skull found in North America to be reconstructed. Many others—some quite old, some more recent—have been sculpted to reveal faces of people from the past who are not often seen and whose stories are rarely told.

History can overlook people for many reasons.

Sometimes people led ordinary lives that were never recorded in any way. Prehistoric people, who lived long before the advent of writing, left behind no written record of their lives, except for symbols or objects painted on cave walls or carved into stone. Even with the invention of writing, most people spent their lives without making a record of what they did, thought, or felt. Without a written account, historians have a harder time knowing what individuals from the past were like.

Sometimes, though, even when written information was available in diaries or journals, church records, court documents, and newspaper accounts, certain people were not respected enough or considered important enough to have their stories told.

And sometimes people were simply erased from history altogether . . .

In 1901, a burial mound containing the remains of more than four hundred Monacan Indians was excavated by an amateur archaeologist. Only a few photos were taken of the excavation, and none of the mound itself. The shadows of the workers and cornstalks were cast on the initial trench, which contained twelve skeletons.

CHAPTER 3

AMOROLECK'S *Ancestors*

CIRCA

1000–1400

No one knows how or when the man and woman died, though it was between six hundred and one thousand years ago. They may have known each other or they may have died centuries apart. When they died, their bodies were placed in a burial mound. Over the years the mound grew as bodies were added. It remained a monument to all who had lived before . . . until the diggers arrived, and then their bones were taken.

In September 1901 an amateur archaeologist named Edward Pleasants Valentine decided to excavate the Hayes Creek Mound, an Indian burial site in Virginia. His father had established a museum in Richmond, Virginia, and Valentine planned to display his finds there.

He instructed his fourteen workers to dig a trench, two feet deep and eight feet wide, around the entire mound. As they did, they uncovered twelve human skeletons. When the trench was complete, the workers "cautiously attacked [the mound] from all sides," hoping to find more burials.

According to Valentine's report, in just a few days

> *more than one hundred skeletons were uncovered and carefully cleaned by means of pocket knives and wisps of broom straw. . . . Accurate memoranda of the location, position, nature, and essential dates were made and photographs taken of the skeletons. . . . The bones allowed to bleach, and hardened by the rays of the sun, were carefully removed and spread upon cotton cloths to dry, after which they were packed in boxes cushioned by crumpled newspapers.*

One of Valentine's fourteen workers, Finley Robson, wrote a letter in which he described what he had seen. The skeletons, he penned, were lying "with their knees close to their face doubled up. . . . It is a great curiosity to everybody. . . . Mr. Valentine says

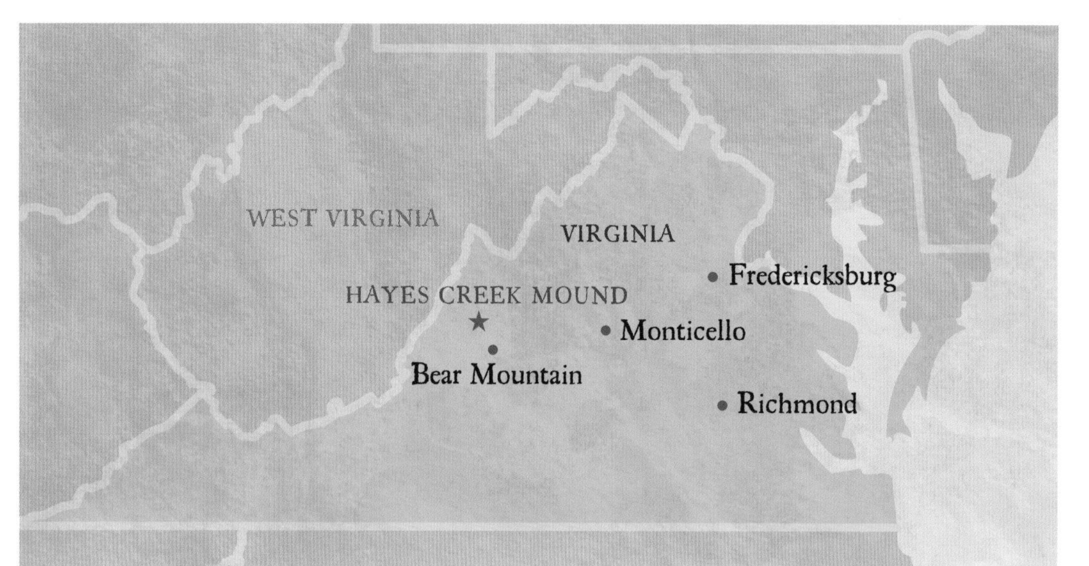

The territory of the Monacan Indians was in central Virginia, far from the coast. They had lived there for many centuries before the English colonists arrived.

Valentine took eighty perfect skulls back to his father's museum in Richmond, Virginia, where he exhibited them.

that he has opened a great many mounds, but he has never got such a good collection of skeletons before. . . . We found two children buried side by side with their faces together. Looked to be 10 or 12 years old."

By the end of the dig, Valentine's workers had unearthed the skeletons of more than four hundred humans and eight dogs. What interested Valentine, however, were the skulls of the dead. He collected eighty of the most perfect skulls he could find, a few "nearly-perfect" skeletons, and the bones of some four hundred Indians who had been buried in the mound. They were then transported to his father's museum. There the skulls were lined up on shelves inside display cases; the skeletons were mostly taken apart, their bones sorted by type and put on view in piles.

Who were the people whose remains Edward Valentine displayed?

No one knew it at the time, but the Hayes Creek Mound and twelve others in Virginia had been built by the Monacans, one of Virginia's first Indian tribes. Between A.D. 800 and 1000, the Monacans migrated from the Ohio Valley to what is now the Piedmont area of Virginia in an attempt to escape their enemies. A Siouan-speaking confederacy that included the Tutelo, Saponi, and Manahoac tribes, among others, they adapted well to their new land. They built towns surrounded by palisades (wooden

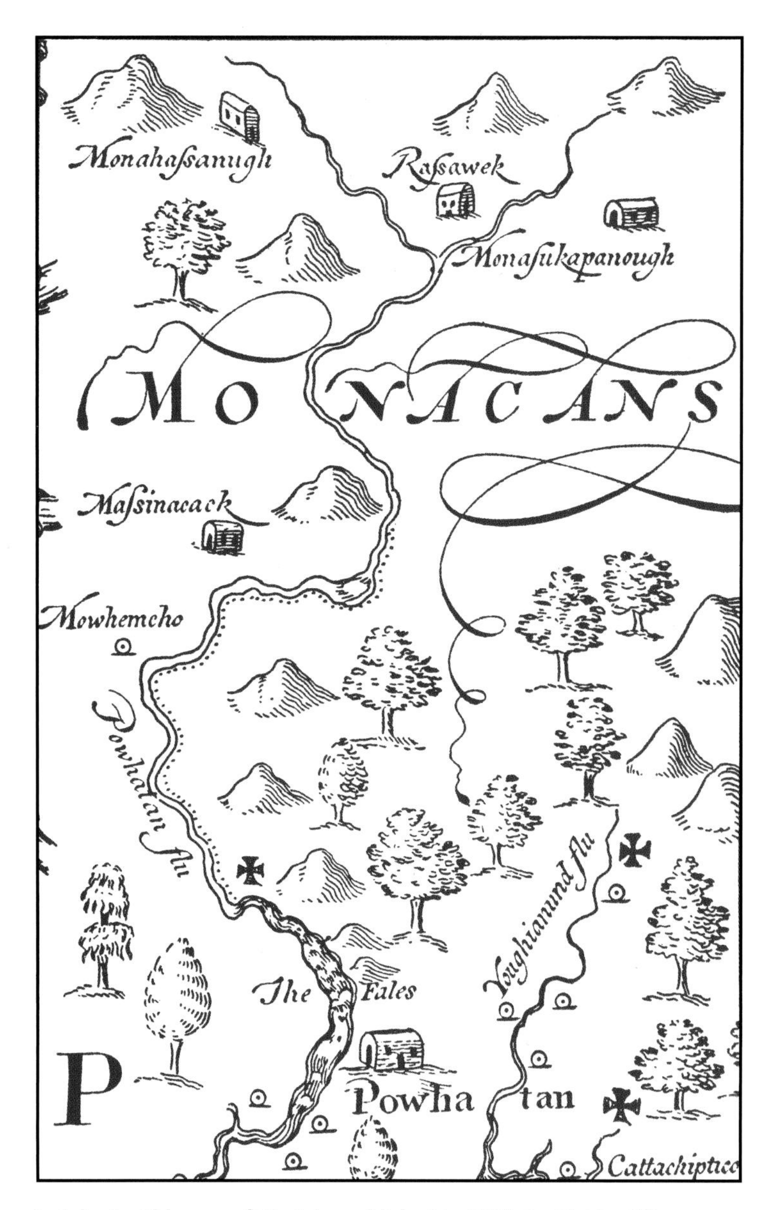

In John Smith's map of Virginia, published in 1612, Smith identifies Monacan territory and towns, far inland from the Powhatans. The map clearly shows that the Monacans were an original Indian tribe in Virginia.

fences). They hunted, fished, and farmed. They mined copper from the Blue Ridge Mountains and traded it for maize, especially to the Algonquin-speaking Powhatans who lived along the Virginia coast. And little by little over the centuries, long before the English colonists arrived, they built at least thirteen burial mounds to honor their dead. A mound, which could be from five to fifteen feet high and more than fifty feet long, might provide a burial place for thousands of people—men, women, and children—from a number of nearby Monacan towns.

When Captain Christopher Newport established the colony of Jamestown in 1607, he encountered the initially friendly Powhatan Indians. Because the Monacans lived far inland, past the fall line on the river, rapids and waterfalls prevented the colonists from sailing upstream into their territory, and the English did not meet them for another year.

That meeting occurred in August 1608, when Captain

John Smith led a group of twelve men on an expedition up the Rappahannock River. The Monacans ambushed the invaders in a hail of arrows. The English returned fire. One Monacan, named Amoroleck, was wounded in the skirmish and taken prisoner. Mosco, a Powhatan interpreter who accompanied the English, wanted to "beat out his brains," but Captain Smith prevented this and had the accompanying doctor treat Amoroleck's injured knee. Then Smith asked him why the Monacans had attacked the English.

Amoroleck replied that the Monacans had heard that the English "were a people come from under the world to take their world from them."

Visitors to Fredericksburg, Virginia, can visit a roadside marker that identifies the general area where Amoroleck was wounded.

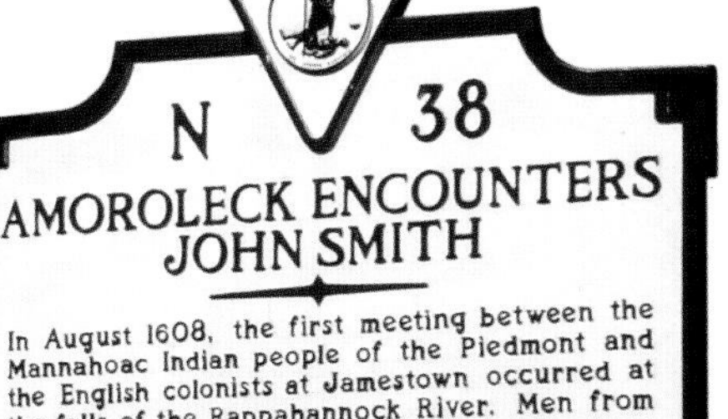

And their world was taken from them.

The Monacans kept their distance from the colonists and other Indian tribes, but war with Iroquois tribes and disease brought by colonists caused their numbers to dwindle. When the colonial settlers encroached on their homeland, they moved farther away, some heading north to Pennsylvania and then to Canada, others moving south, where they joined with other tribes. A small community of Monacans remained in Virginia in an isolated area around Bear Mountain that had been part of their original homeland. Eventually, other settlers came to live near Bear Mountain, and over time some Monacans intermarried with their neighbors.

By the 1800s, most people in Virginia knew nothing of the Monacans and thought of the mounds only as "Indian mounds"; they were up for grabs by settlers who wanted to cultivate them. In 1788, Thomas Jefferson examined one of the mounds, called Indian Grave, which was only two miles from his home at Monticello. At first Jefferson dug into it at a few random places and "came to collections of human bones, at different depths . . . [that] were lying in the utmost confusion, some vertical . . . some horizontal, and directed to every point of the compass, entangled and held together in clusters by the earth."

To investigate further, he cut an opening into the middle of the

"Amoroleck's Words" by Karenne Wood

The writer, anthropologist, and Monacan historian Karenne Wood stands in front of the Episcopal mission school near Bear Mountain that is now the ancestral museum of the Monacan Indian Nation.

You must have been a sight,
Captain John Smith,
as your dugout approached,
with Jamestown's men
sporting plumed hats,
poufed knickers, beards, stockings,
funny little shoes.
You might have looked, to us,
well,
uncivilized.
We fought you, we know,
because you wrote it down.
One man was left behind. Wounded.
At your mercy. Among your shining goods—
mirrors, knives, firearms, glass beads—
where was mercy? Maybe you left it
in England. Eager to learn, Captain Smith,
you asked about the worlds he knew,
whether there was gold,
why his people had fought
when you came to them "in love."
He told you in his dialect,
which no one now speaks.
You recorded his name. His words.
Not his fate.
Of all the words our people spoke
in the year of your Lord 1608,
only his answer remains:
"We heard that you were a people
come from under the world,
to take our world from us."

mound, which revealed four layers of bones separated by rocks and earth. He wrote in his book *Notes on the State of Virginia* that the "bones nearest the surface were least decayed. No holes were discovered in any of them, as if made with bullets, arrows, or other weapons. I conjectured that in this [mound] might have been a thousand skeletons."

Jefferson had no idea that he had partly excavated a burial mound used by the Monacans, and neither did Edward Valentine in 1901 when his workers dug the Hayes Creek Mound. Not until the 1980s did researchers come to understand who built the thirteen burial mounds and whose bodies they contained. In 1990, with the Native American Graves Protection and Repatriation Act about to be passed, the Valentine Museum transferred the Hayes Creek remains to the Virginia Department of Historic Resources (DHR), which was charged with returning them to any affiliated tribe for reburial.

These remains, the DHR realized, were of Monacan ancestry, and in 1998 they were repatriated to the remaining members of the tribe. Instead of the bones of four hundred individuals, though, the Valentine Museum had given the DHR only twenty-one cardboard boxes that contained forty-eight skulls and twenty-five hundred bones and bone fragments—the jumbled remains of only about one hundred individuals.

Where were the other three hundred individuals that E. P. Valentine had disinterred? No one knew, but many were concerned that the missing bones had been taken as souvenirs long before and even displayed as artifacts in private homes.

Although the Monacans wanted to bury their ancestors in the tribe's cemetery on Bear Mountain, they also wanted to take the opportunity to learn as much as they could about them. They were especially interested in having facial reconstructions done not only to see what their ancestors looked like but to bring their history to life. They had only a few photos of Monacans from the early 1900s; no historical drawings, paintings, or other illustrations of Monacans were known to exist. The reconstructions would help fill a large void.

The anthropologist Debra Gold examined the bones and concluded that the Monacans were in generally good health. Their most prevalent health issue was related to their teeth. About 30 percent of the 437 teeth found in the boxes contained cavities, though most were not severe; these were most likely caused by eating maize. Then she advised Monacan officials of three skulls that would work for facial reconstruction. Eventually, they chose two—one male and one female.

No one knows where the two people were buried in Hayes Creek Mound. Gold determined that the woman was between thirty-eight and forty-eight when she died; the man was between thirty-five and fifty-five years old. Because their skulls and bones were separated by Valentine, Gold could not tell anything else about them individually.

After she was contacted by the tribe, the sculptor Sharon Long spent a year researching the Monacans and then sculpting the faces. When she was finished, she told the reporter Carlos Santos that she believed the faces were about 90 percent accurate. She made one change when she noticed a birth defect on the nasal area of the woman's skull. Because the reconstructions were going to be exhibited in the tribe's museum, Long corrected the deformity.

Of course, the expression on a sculpted face can be influenced by the artist. Long admitted that the two Monacans looked a bit melancholy, a deliberate decision on her part: "They were in wars . . . they were always watching for predators, trying to get food, fighting the cold."

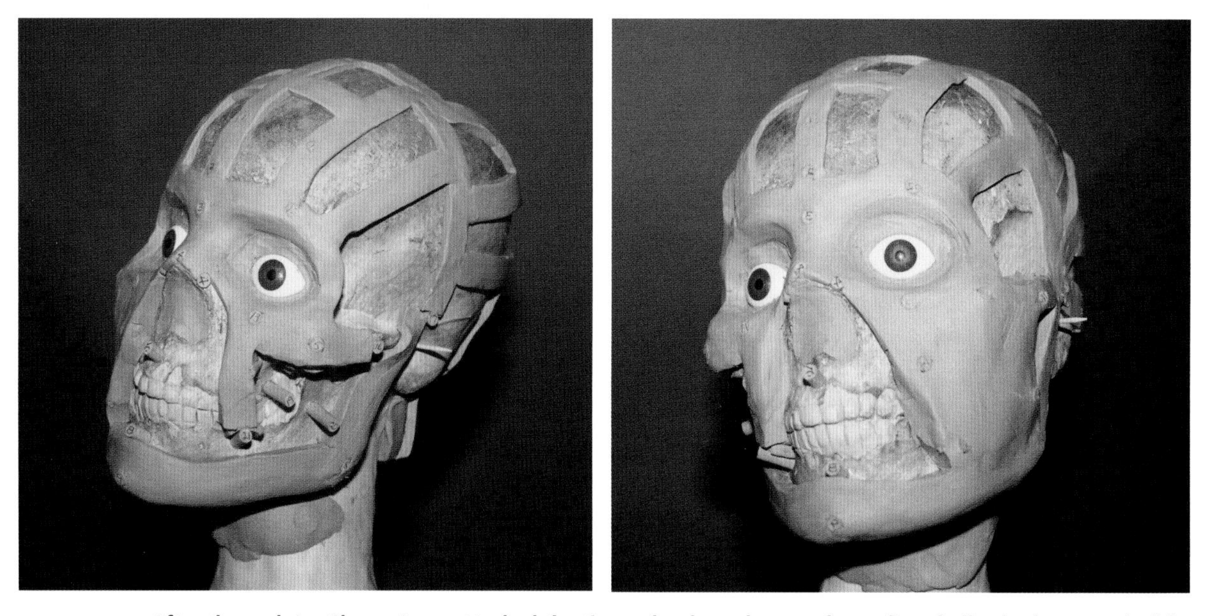

After the sculptor Sharon Long attached the tissue-depth markers to the replica skulls, she began to build the faces of the two Monacan Indians with clay strips (above). When the faces were finished she made a mold of each so that she could cast them in a more durable product. She unfolded the heads, then painted the faces and added wigs to make them look more lifelike.

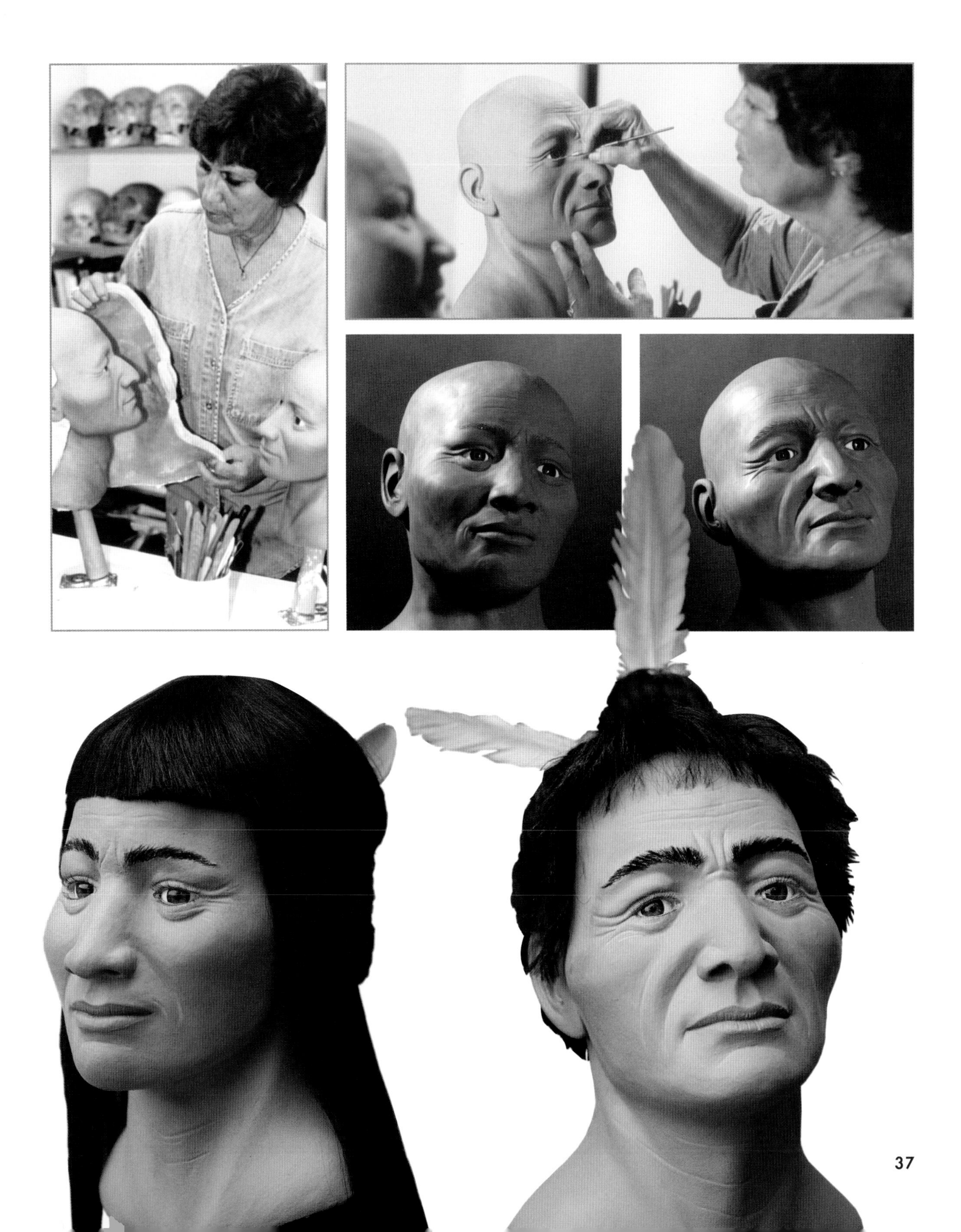

When the two reconstructions were placed on display in the Monacan Ancestral Museum near Bear Mountain, tribal members came to get a glimpse of what their ancestors had looked like. Many were struck by their resemblance to present-day Monacans.

Not long afterward, on October 8, 2000, the skeletons that had been taken from the Hayes Creek Mound were reburied in the cemetery on Bear Mountain. Tribal members prepared the remains by wrapping them in red cloth. Then one hundred small bundles were carefully placed in the bottom of a ten-foot-square grave, along with gourds and baskets containing food and drink. Then the grave was filled in and mounded with earth.

The ancestors of Amoroleck had come home to Bear Mountain.

At the 2010 Monacan Nation Powwow near Amherst, Virginia, Jessica Turpin (left) and Quinton Talbott posed for formal portraits.

The cemetery on Bear Mountain is a sacred place to the Monacan Indian Nation. The remains from the Hayes Creek Mound are buried under the rocks on the left. When tribal members visit the grave, they often place a sacred rock atop it to commemorate their visit.

Erasing the Monacans

From 1908 until 1963, the only education that Monacan children living in Virginia could receive was provided by the Episcopal mission school near Bear Mountain. These photographs of the school and some of its students were taken around 1914 by Jackson Davis, an educator devoted to improving the quality of schools for people of color in the southeastern United States.

Considered a lost tribe by many, the Monacans found themselves—along with other Virginia Indian tribes—being erased from the state's history in the twentieth century. In 1924 the Virginia legislature passed the Racial Integrity Act, which required anyone born in Virginia to have a birth certificate classifying the person's race; the act named the possible races as "Caucasian, negro, Mongolian, American Indian, Asiatic Indian, Malay, or any mixture thereof."

In effect, the act divided the citizens of Virginia into two groups: whites and all others, who were seen as "colored." By classifying each individual's race, the act sought to prevent any intermarriage between whites and people of color: "It shall hereafter be unlawful for any white person in this State to marry any save a white person." Local authorities were told not to grant marriage licenses until they had verified the racial identity of the two people.

The law had a particularly devastating impact on the Monacans because of a man named Walter A. Plecker, the director of Virginia's Bureau of Vital Statistics. Charged with upholding the law, Plecker believed that the "Indian race" in Virginia no longer existed. He did everything in his power to make certain that birth certificates that listed "Indian" were changed to "negro."

Plecker wrote many letters to Virginians threatening them for failing to comply with

the law. In one, he addressed a woman whose child had been labeled as white on her birth certificate when Plecker believed she was not. "This is to give you warning that this is a mulatto child and you cannot pass it off as white . . . ," he wrote. "You will have to do something about this matter and see that this child is not allowed to mix with white children." He even went so far as to order the removal of people buried in "white cemeteries" if he believed they had "mixed" ancestry.

Plecker took a particular dislike to the Monacans still in Virginia—the community living around Bear Mountain. He considered them neither white nor black, referring to them as "mongrels." He developed a "hit list" of Monacan family names and sent it to various state agencies. The names on the list included Branham, Johns, Clark, Hamilton, Roberts, and Wood. Anyone whose name was on the list was not allowed to marry a white person or even associate with whites. Many of the remaining Monacans

Monacan children await the start of their tribe's annual powwow in May 2011 near Amherst, Virginia.

moved away from Virginia to escape this racist law and Plecker's wrath.

The eight hundred or so Monacans who stayed behind in Virginia were, Plecker wrote in a letter, "giving us the most trouble, through . . . persistent claims of being Indians. Some well-meaning church workers have established an 'Indian Mission' around which they rally."

The mission, established near Bear Mountain by the Episcopal Church in 1908, also provided a school for Monacan children, the only school they were able to attend. Because of the Racial Integrity Act, they were allowed to attend black schools, where "they were no more welcome than in white schools. Most simply refused . . . and instead attended the six-grade school at St. Paul's Mission at the foot of Bear Mountain."

The school was cited for overcrowding and sanitation problems, but the students didn't mind. One former student later recalled, "When we were coming to school here, . . . this was just heaven. We had the best times, the best teachers, best missionary workers." Still, if Monacan children wished to continue their education after sixth grade, they were forced to leave the state.

The Racial Integrity Act remained in effect until 1967, when the Supreme Court found that it violated the equal protection clause of the Fourteenth Amendment to the Constitution. A year later it was repealed by the Virginia General Assembly. Three years after that, in 1971, the first Monacan students graduated from public high school in Virginia.

Even today, though, the effects of the Racial Integrity Act linger. The two-thousand-member Monacan Indian Nation has not received federal recognition as an American Indian tribe. To qualify for this designation, the Monacans must prove that the tribe has existed continuously since 1900. Because Plecker and others helped to erase their history, the tribe has had difficulty finding accurate records that show their existence. But the Monacans are not alone. Seven other Virginia Indian tribes are awaiting federal recognition as well.

La Salle claimed the Mississippi and its surrounding land for the king of France, Louis XIV, in this illustration by the French artist Edy LeGrand.

CHAPTER 4

A STRANDED SAILOR *from France*

The sailor was a long way from home—across the ocean in a new land—when he died a horrible, thirsty death. His body was curled into a ball surrounded by coils of rope that had been tied to the ship's anchor. Not long afterward, the ship sank in a shallow bay and was covered with a thick layer of mud. When archaeologists discovered the shipwreck more than three hundred years later, they found it was a treasure trove of information about life in the last part of the 1600s. It was also the sailor's coffin . . .

On April 9, 1682, the French explorer René-Robert Cavelier, Sieur de La Salle, arrived at the mouth of the Mississippi River; he was the first European to explore its length. He planted a cross and a French flag in the soil and claimed the river and all the lands that bordered it for the French king, Louis XIV.

Later that year, after he had returned to France, he asked the king for permission to begin a French colony on the Mississippi. Louis XIV approved the funding, and two years later, La Salle set sail from France with some three hundred people: sailors, soldiers, and future colonists. His four ships, armed with cannons to defend against pirates, were filled with building materials, supplies, and trading goods.

Despite La Salle's grand plan and best intentions, the mission was plagued with problems. First, as the convoy of four ships reached Santo Domingo in the Caribbean Sea, Spanish pirates captured the smallest vessel. Then La Salle and the other two ships unknowingly missed the mouth of the Mississippi, making landfall on January 17, 1685, some four hundred miles to the west. Aware of his mistake, he established a temporary camp on an island near the entrance to what is now called Matagorda Bay, along the Gulf of Mexico. But shortly after their arrival, his largest ship, *L'Aimable,* ran aground on a sandbank. The crew tried to rescue its provisions by ferrying them to shore on small boats. But heavy seas caused the ship to break up one night, sending the better part of the colonists' supplies adrift. Finally, in March, the captain of the third ship, named *Le Joly,* announced that he was ready to return to France, now that he had completed his assigned mission of accompanying La Salle and helping him unload his cargo.

La Salle's expedition missed the mouth of the Mississippi and landed instead in what is now Matagorda Bay on the Gulf coast of Texas.

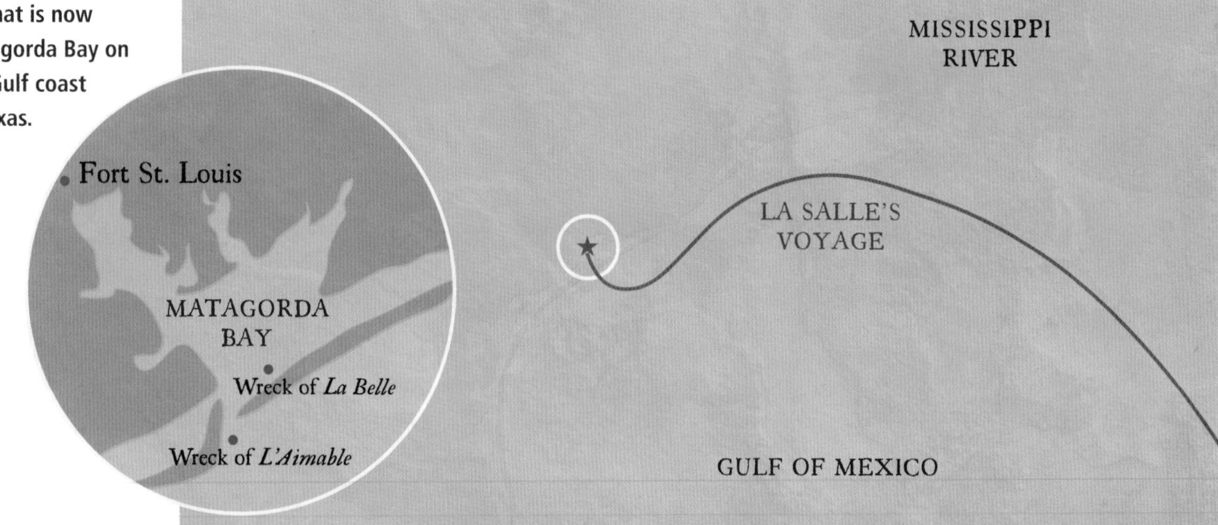

One of La Salle's boats, *La Belle,* was built in a dry dock similar to this one, in Rochefort, France, in 1684.

Unfortunately, many of the people on board the remaining two ships, now disillusioned and demoralized, wanted to return with him.

In the end, La Salle was left with one small ship—named *La Belle*—and 180 people. To survive, they built a temporary fort for protection from the Karankawa Indians, but La Salle managed its construction badly. Fort St. Louis was only one main building with four rooms: one for La Salle, one for his priests, another for officers, and a fourth for supplies. All other colonists lived in five makeshift houses, their walls formed from wooden stakes covered with mud and their roofs from animal hides.

By summer, about half of the colonists had died, many from disease. Some—including the captain of *La Belle*—had even died from eating prickly pear cactus fruits without removing the needles; their throats swelled from the injury, and they suffocated. The crew of *La Belle* also suffered many deaths and debilitating illness. The sailors who remained on board were barely enough to sail the ship.

With no means of returning everyone to France and with no desire to be known as a failure, La Salle was intent on trying to find the Mississippi. After one failed attempt in the fall, he tried again in January 1686, placing most of the remaining supplies on *La*

Belle and heading off over land with twenty men. He ordered the crew to anchor on the north end of Matagorda Bay and wait for his return in ten days. La Salle gave them just enough food and water to last two weeks.

But La Salle did not return as he promised, and for almost a month the crew of *La Belle* struggled to survive. As their water supplies dwindled, the captain ordered his five best sailors to take the only boat they had and row to shore to replenish their water. They loaded empty casks onto the boat and shoved off. When they tried to return later that day, strong winds blew them back. The crew implored the captain to light a torch and position it atop the ship's mast, so that the men in the boat could find their way back to *La Belle* that night. The captain, however, would only place a candle in a lantern, which the winds quickly snuffed. In the morning, the five men and their boat were nowhere to be seen.

La Salle's landing site at Matagorda Bay was imagined in this 1698 engraving by the artist Michael Vander Gucht as a lush rainforest rather than a flat, swampy terrain.

Now everyone aboard *La Belle* was trapped. The remaining crew not only ran out of water but without the small boat had no way to retrieve any; like many sailors at the time, they could not swim. Several men soon died of dehydration, their bodies left on board.

The crew desperately tried to survive by slaughtering the eight pigs they had and making bread from flour and seawater. Finally, they set sail, hoping to reach the colonists at Fort St. Louis. On the way, the ship encountered a storm and ran aground on a sandbank. Two sailors rigged together a makeshift raft but drowned after the planks separated. Eventually, other sailors constructed a

The Final Days of La Salle and His Colony

In January 1687, La Salle left Fort St. Louis for the third time, hoping to find Indians who would help the few remaining colonists. Instead, after journeying for two months, some of the men in his party plotted to murder him.

According to a journal written by Henri Joutel, one of La Salle's loyal lieutenants, one conspirator hid in some tall grass on March 19, 1687, and fired his musket at La Salle. "The shot hit La Salle in the head; he fell dead in place, without uttering a word. . . . When the assassins were gathered, they plundered the [body of] La Salle as a final cruelty, stripping him of even his shirt . . . and dragged his body into the brush where they left it to the discretion of wolves and other wild animals."

Eventually, Joutel and four survivors from the group managed to make their way to Canada, where they boarded a ship bound for France. Instead of requesting help for the colonists from the French colony in Canada, though, they waited until they arrived in France in November 1688.

By then, any help would have arrived too late. In January 1689, the colony was attacked by the Karankawa Indians, and all of the colonists, except for five children, were massacred.

La Salle and three of his loyal followers were murdered by five of his men in March 1687 near what is now Navasota, Texas. The artist Ludwell Sheppard depicted the death in this 1881 illustration.

better raft and made their way to a narrow strip of land where they could camp. It took three months for the only six survivors of *La Belle* to reach Fort St. Louis.

A month later La Salle finally returned, without having found the mouth of the Mississippi.

Although La Salle's colony was a failure, his expeditions played an important role in the history of the United States. Over the years, many archaeologists have tried to find sites associated with La Salle, but a marine archaeologist named Barto Arnold wanted to find the shipwreck of *La Belle.*

In 1995, using a magnetometer, which measures the earth's magnetic field, Arnold and his team surveyed areas of Matagorda Bay to detect any magnetic distortions. These distortions—called anomalies—could indicate the presence of iron, a possible sign of a shipwreck. That June, the team found thirty-nine anomalies in the search area. Arnold analyzed each one and ranked them based on the whether they might indicate the presence of *La Belle.*

On the morning of July 5, after anchoring their ship above the most promising anomaly, the first team of divers dropped into the shallow waters. They had no idea what they would find, but given the murkiness of the water, they knew they would not be able to see it. They would have to use their hands, to feel for any signs of a shipwreck.

Soon they surfaced with the news that the anomaly was a shipwreck covered with mud. To find out if it was *La Belle,* they had to remove the mud. They did this by directing the powerful current from one of the boat's propellers through a pipe aimed toward the wreck.

By noon they had uncovered wooden boards, marble-size musket balls, and a bronze buckle. Then came an astounding discovery: a sediment-encrusted cannon with ornate designs. Although Arnold and his team sensed that they had found the French shipwreck, they had to wait a few weeks until the 793-pound cannon could be salvaged. The crowd of waiting archaeologists and reporters saw that the cannon sported the words LE COMTE DE VERMANDOIS (the Count of Vermandois). The count was a son of Louis XIV, La Salle's king. The cannon provided the necessary proof that *La Belle* had been discovered after 309 years.

Once *La Belle* had been identified, archaeologists had to decide how to excavate

it. Normally, a shipwreck is uncovered by divers rather slowly, often only in warmer months and over a number of years; the unexcavated portions of the wreck are left in the ocean until the next excavation season. But treasure hunters would be interested in looting whatever remained behind. To speed up the recovery of the vessel, officials decided to build a cofferdam around the ship. This metal enclosure would allow marine archaeologists to pump the water out so that the shipwreck could be excavated drily and more easily from the top down.

Once the cofferdam was completed, in August 1996, archaeologists went to work. They quickly discovered that the ship had sunk almost completely intact. It had settled onto the bottom with its cargo still resting in the hold. Then a thick layer of mud settled onto the ship, which enabled its contents to be unusually well preserved.

A cofferdam with two concentric walls was built to enable archaeologists to excavate *La Belle.* The walls were pounded forty feet into the bottom of the bay; the thirty-three-foot space between them was filled with sand to slow any leaks.

Once the cofferdam was completed, sump pumps removed the water from the center, revealing the bottom of Matagorda Bay and the outlines of *La Belle*. To avoid any destruction, archaeologists excavated the wreck while lying on the boards positioned across it.

As they removed the mud, they discovered a treasure trove of historical items in the ship's hold that were meant to start a new colony in North America.

La Belle, though, held more than objects. In October 1996, when the archaeologists had excavated their way into the bow, they found a large coil of anchor rope and bunks for some of the crew. The rope was so fragile that they could only remove it in short sections. In the middle of the coil they discovered the skeleton of a man. He lay face-down near a small cask that had once contained water. Archaeologists suspect that he died of dehydration before *La Belle* ran aground.

Any other human remains from a shipwreck might have decomposed and vanished forever, but mud had encased the ship in an oxygen-free tomb. Without oxygen, bacteria couldn't eat away at the wooden ship and its contents. The man's body—along with clues to his tragic death—had been preserved for more than three hundred years.

But there was more.

Besides the empty cask, a small pewter cup, called a porringer, was

At the end of the excavation, the empty hull of *La Belle* was revealed, along with the round stub of its mast. Archaeologists then had to tag each timber so that it could be disassembled and taken ashore where the timbers would be preserved for reassembly.

How to Start a Colony

Among the more unusual items found in the wreckage were ceramic firepots (center), which could be used like hand grenades to defend the sailors against close enemy attack. To use it, sailors would fill the firepot with some type of flammable liquid, place a grenade (left) with its wooden fuse into the pot, and cover the pot with a fused lid (right). Next they would light the fuse and throw it at the nearby vessel.

Altogether, some one million artifacts were uncovered from *La Belle*, many of them contained in eighty-five barrels. The barrels had held liquids (water and wine, for example); tar and other sealants for repairing the ship; gunpowder; brass pots and cooking utensils; pewter plates; and many types of weapons, including muskets, knives, axe heads, and nine firepots, a type of bomb that would have been used against attacking ships. The largest number of items, though, were the goods intended for trading with Indian tribes: about 750,000 glass seed beads, 16,000 brass pins, 1,600 copper rings, and 1,300 brass bells.

Archaeologists were stunned to find the skeleton of a man on the coiled anchor rope in the bow of the ship. An empty cask of water can be seen to his right.

Archaeologists carefully removed the remains so that they could be studied to find out more about the person.

found near the skeleton. On its side, a name had been stamped: C. BARANGE. Suddenly the nameless sailor who had died so many years earlier had perhaps been identified.

Whether this was the sailor's name or not, though, the anthropologist Gentry Steele of Texas A&M University studied his bones to learn more about him. They indicated that he was about forty years old when he died. At the time of his death his right ankle was badly sprained, and he had terrible abscesses in his mouth caused by cavities. His skull revealed that his nose had been broken, possibly in a fistfight with a right-handed opponent. One leg was shorter than the other. His back showed the effects of too much heavy lifting. And tooth loss from his abscesses had meant that he could chew food only with his front teeth.

Although researchers hoped to use his DNA to determine whether he had living relatives, they were unable to extract a large-enough sample from his bones and teeth. What they could do, however, was

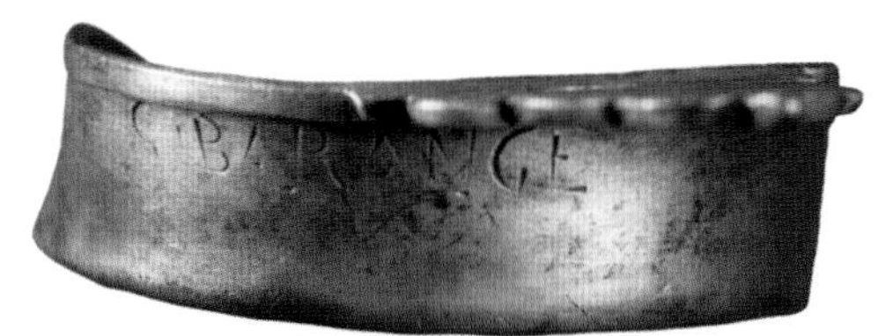

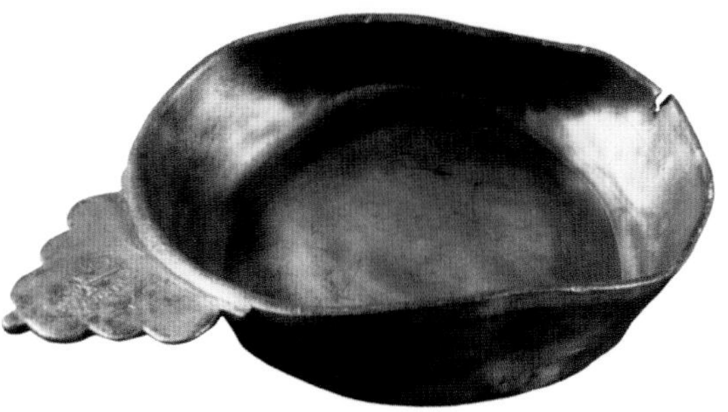

The pewter cup was intended to be used for wine tasting. Engraved on the cup (top) was the name C. Barange.

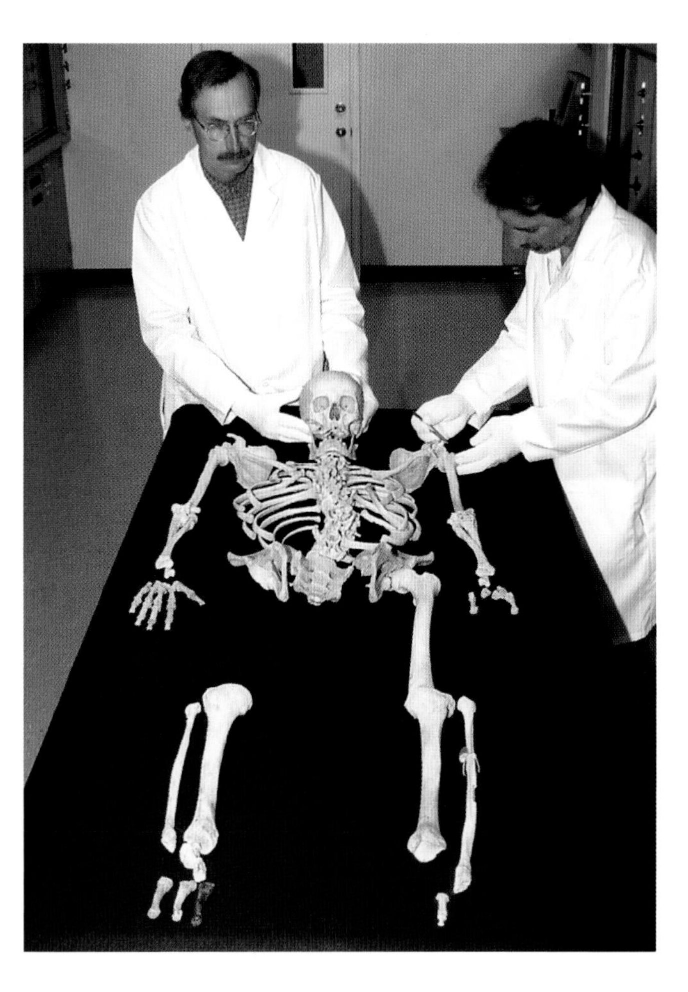

By laying out the bones of the man, anthropologists were able to determine some facts about his life. Here James Bruseth (left), who directed the project, and the archaeologist Jeff Durst inspect the sailor's remains.

show the world what the man had looked like. They made a CT scan of Barange's skull and created an exact copy of his skull in resin.

The replica was sent to the sculptor Amanda Danning, who had reconstructed the faces of many skulls over the years, especially for the Smithsonian Institution. Danning took the replica skull and began applying clay. In two days' time, a forgotten French sailor who died a horrible death was revealed in Danning's recreation of his face.

This man may well have been a thirsty sailor whose last name was Barange.

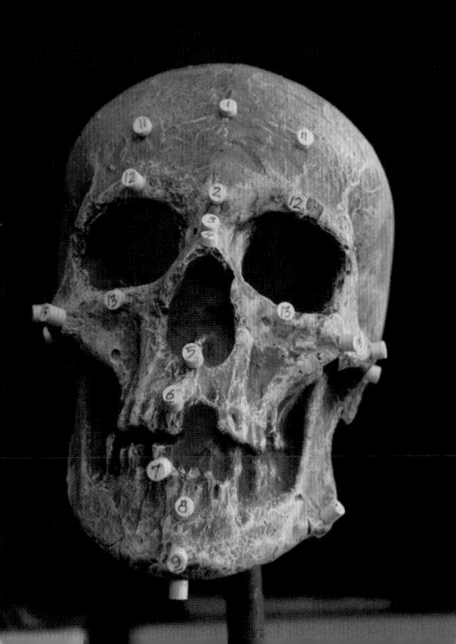

The sculptor Amanda Danning reconstructed the face of C. Barange. After placing tissue-depth markers onto a copy of the skull (left), she applied gray clay to approximate the muscle groups of the face (top left and top right). Her worktable (above left) includes many tools, a copy of the skull for reference, and a Crock-Pot to make the clay more pliable.

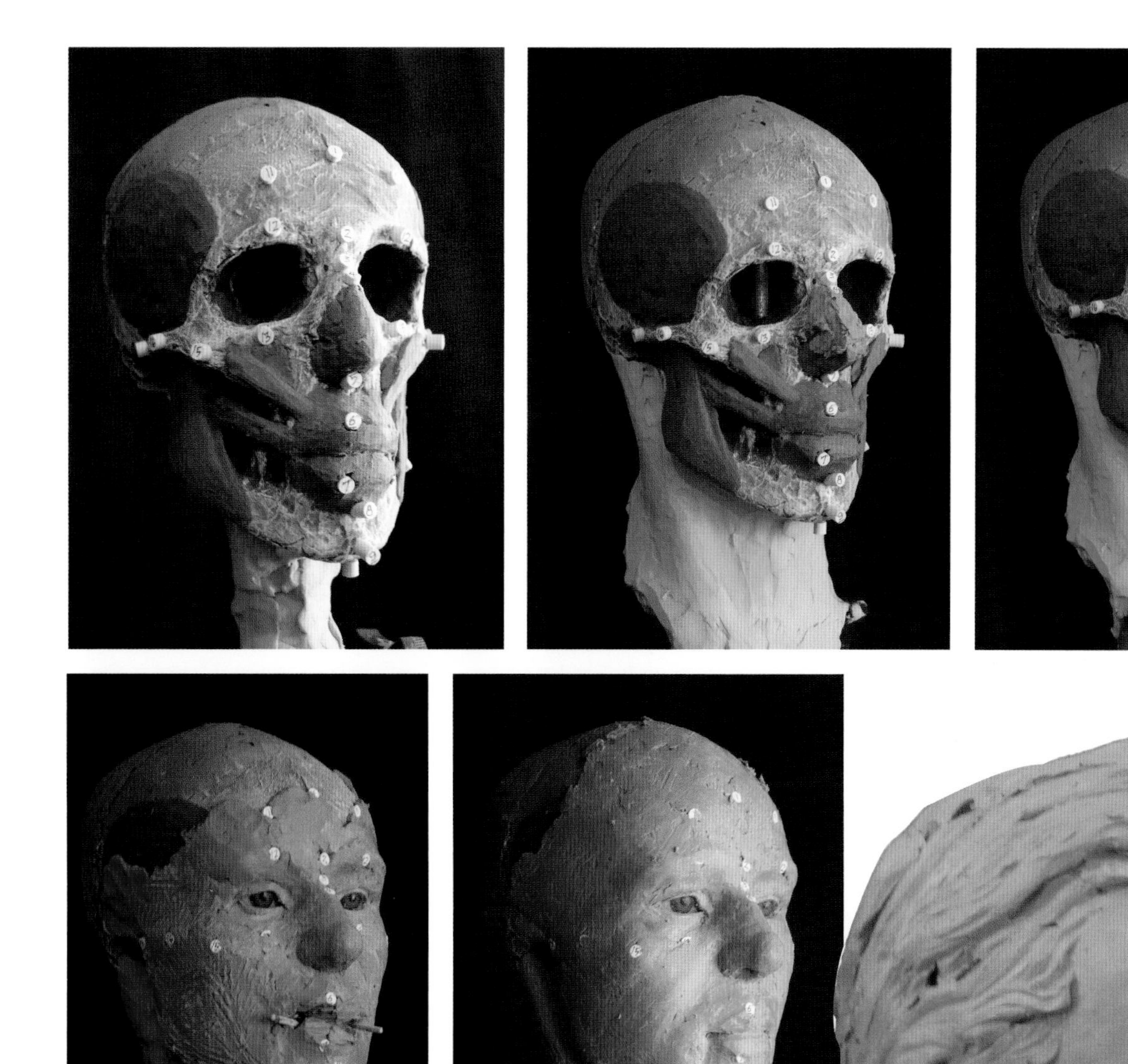

Over the course of two days, Danning created Barange's face. The final face will be displayed in the Bob Bullock Texas State History Museum in Austin.

RENE ROBERT CAVELIER
SIEUR DE LA SALLE

On February 3, 2004, the remains of C. Barange were buried in the Texas State Cemetery in Austin, above.

A monument honoring La Salle is located near the site of his first camp on the shores of Matagorda Bay.

At the corner of Pearl and Howard Streets in Albany, New York, archaeologists excavated a small area in 1998, hoping to discover information about Albany's colonial past.

CHAPTER 5

PEARL from Colonial New York

She had spent her life working hard. At death she had infections and abscesses, a painful left leg, and gout in both feet. She was buried in the Lutheran burying ground on Pearl Street, but if any record of her burial existed, it was lost over time. And when the burying ground was later relocated, the woman's coffin was forgotten beneath the ever-expanding city of Albany.

In 1998 the New York State Department of Transportation (DOT) decided to improve Pearl Street, a major thoroughfare in downtown Albany. As part of the planning process, the DOT contracted archaeologists from the New York State Museum to perform a survey of the construction area, as required by federal law, to determine whether any historical artifacts or human remains might be uncovered by workers. Because Pearl Street had played an important role in Albany since the early seventeenth century, the head archaeologist Chuck Fisher reported that the entire street was likely to yield any number of archaeological discoveries. This meant that an archaeologist would have to be on site during construction to examine anything that turned up.

One archaeological "hot spot," Fisher determined, was at the corner of Pearl and Howard Streets, which had been the site of the Lutheran church, its parsonage, and its burying ground (or cemetery) in colonial times. This corner was scheduled for a drainpipe installation later during the construction schedule. When Fisher submitted his archaeology plan for monitoring the construction, he requested permission to excavate the corner during the first few months.

Albany was originally a Dutch settlement named Beverwyck before it was taken over by the English in 1664 and renamed.

His plan was approved. At the same time that construction began, archaeologists began to excavate the corner of Pearl and Howard. After several weeks of routine digging, they uncovered a section of wooden planks that, they believed, formed part of the floor of the early Lutheran parsonage.

Curious to see what might lie below the floorboards, the archaeologists wanted to keep digging. But the five-foot-deep excavation trench was seeping water, which made it unsafe to dig deeper by hand. A backhoe would have to be used for any further excavation, and the team would have to stand on the sidewalk and watch as it safely scooped up slurry, or watery dirt, and dumped it onto the pavement.

On April 24, 1998, the backhoe excavation began. After the backhoe operator dumped the first scoop of slurry onto the pavement, Nancy Davis, the archaeologist who supervised the dig, inspected the contents and found only mud. But the next scoop, Davis noticed immediately, contained some small pieces of wood embedded in the muddy clay. Then a round object about "the size of a large grapefruit," Davis later recalled, cascaded out with the mud and rolled to her feet. She automatically reached down and retrieved it . . . then realized that she was holding a human skull. The backhoe had hit a coffin from the old Lutheran burying ground—a surprise, since city records indicated that the cemetery had been moved to a new location in 1786!

The first excavation shaft revealed a triangular section of the floorboards of the Lutheran parsonage. Archaeologists continued digging to see what was beneath the parsonage.

When human remains are discovered at a work site, certain protocols must be followed to make sure that federal and state laws are not broken. Davis halted the excavation immediately, then called her boss, Chuck Fisher, to report the find. Next, the police and coroner were notified, so that they could officially determine whether a crime had occurred. Soon afterward, Fisher arrived with a bioarchaeologist from the New York State Museum. She took a look at the remains—a skull

The Lutherans of Albany

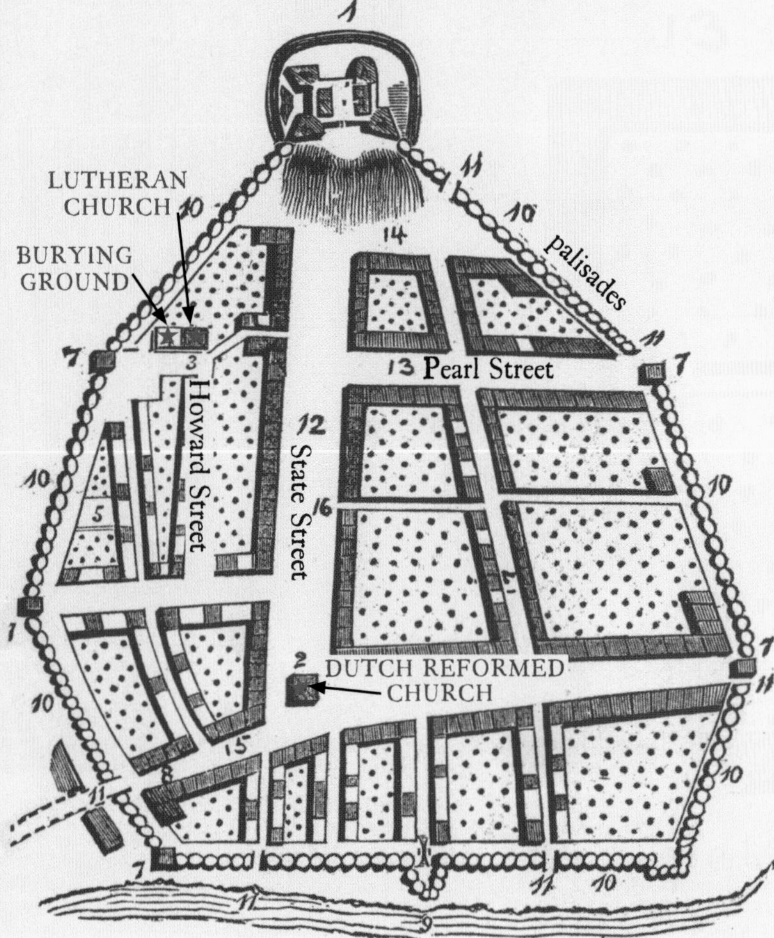

This 1695 map shows the area of Albany within its palisades. A narrow extension of Pearl Street, shown to the left of State Street, was home to the Lutheran church and its burying ground.

The main church of the Dutch and English colony was the Dutch Reformed church, which was positioned prominently in the town. This illustration is of the second church, built in 1715 and relocated in 1806.

The First Lutheran Church of Albany was little more than a house when it was built in 1677 next to the Lutheran burying ground, surrounded by a large field at the end of Pearl Street. Its construction was an important step in religious freedom in the British colony of New York.

The church had not been welcomed during the Dutch rule of Albany. When Scandinavian, German, and French settlers wished to practice their Lutheran religion beginning in 1649, Dutch leaders refused to let them worship, have a minister, or build a church. At that time, only the Dutch Reformed religion was permitted, and anyone who was found practicing another religion would receive a heavy fine or other punishment. In 1656, when a Lutheran man tried to lead sixteen people in worship in a private house, he was arrested.

After the British took over the colony in 1664, however, they gave the Lutherans permission to worship, as long as they pledged their allegiance to the British. In 1669, the Lutherans held their first service. In 1670, they bought some land on Pearl Street, which they used first for a burying ground, adding their first church about 1677.

and mandible broken by the backhoe—and told Fisher and Davis that the skull belonged to a female of European ancestry.

Two days later, representatives from the police department, the mayor's and the coroner's offices, the transportation department, and the archaeology team met to decide what to do. Should construction be stopped until the burial was completely removed? Or should the undisturbed portion of the burial stay in place so that construction could continue as scheduled? In the end, all agreed to excavate the now headless woman so that her remains could be reburied somewhere else.

To avoid further damage to the burial, the archaeology team had to dig by hand. First, though, workers widened and reinforced the excavation shaft so that it would not collapse; they also installed a sump pump to remove any water that collected. When this was done, each team member took a turn at the bottom of the shaft, scooping up buckets of mud and passing them to others at street level.

At one point, a crew member named Joel Ross was working at the bottom of the shaft when his foot unexpectedly broke through the earth and he found himself standing in water up to his ankle. The crew wondered if he had stepped into an old wooden drain used in colonial times. After removing his foot from the hole, Ross reached into the murky water until he felt an object. He grasped it and extracted something long, thin, and covered with mud. When members of the crew saw what he was holding, they told him that it was a leg bone; he dropped it immediately.

Ross had found the coffin.

Although the woman's skull was shattered into many pieces by the backhoe, it was still considered to be in good condition.

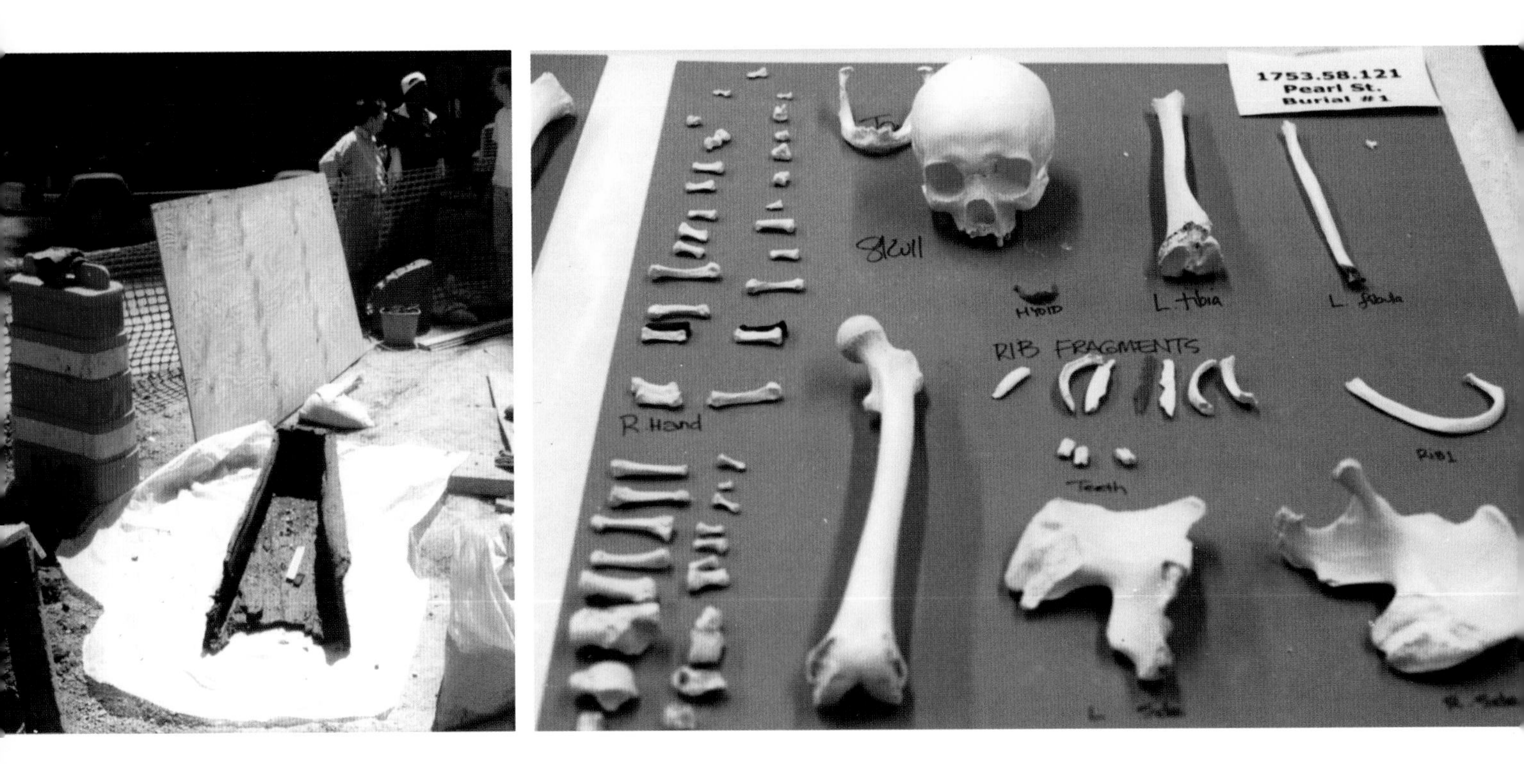

The coffin, partially deteriorated over the centuries, held the body of a woman from colonial Albany.

When anthropologists at the New York State Museum pieced together the woman's skeleton, they were able to see what kind of life she had led by signs in her bones.

Late into that night, the team worked to uncover the rest of the coffin and remove the bones. They wrapped each one in acid-free paper to prevent any decay or contamination, placed the bones in boxes, and sent them to the anthropology lab at the New York State Museum. Later, when they cleaned the skeleton and laid it on an examination table, the scientists wondered who the woman was and what her life had been like. Then, as bioarchaeologists examined her skeleton, her bones began to tell part of her story.

When she died, the woman was five feet one inch tall and in her early forties. Pieces of stoneware recovered in the dirt above her coffin indicated that she had been buried in the mid-1700s, most likely about the year 1742.

Her skeleton clearly showed signs that her life had been very difficult. Many bones had lesions, or abnormalities, which indicated that she had suffered many physical illnesses, including sinus and lung infections, a chronic inflammation of her lower left leg, and gout. She had lost over half of her teeth long before her death, thanks in part to a high-starch diet. Of the seven heavily tartared teeth that remained, six showed signs of severe decay. Bioarchaeologists could not determine a definite cause of her death, however. They speculated that, with her immune system weakened by infections and abscesses, she might have died of pneumonia or a terrible influenza.

Before long, this nameless woman became known as Pearl, for the street under which she was found.

What was colonial Albany like? During Pearl's lifetime, Albany was a military center for the British colony of New York. It housed a fort as well as a thriving community of fur traders, farmers, and businesspeople. A census taken in the mid-1700s counted a population of more than 4,000 individuals, living in some 335 households. The town was surrounded by a wooden palisade (protective fence); livestock such as cows and pigs lived within the walls as well. One visitor to Albany in the mid-1700s observed that "each

The hole made by Joel Ross's boot after it plunged through the bottom of the excavation shaft is visible to the right of the red and white marker.

Forgetting Pearl

The archaeologists Chuck Fisher and Nancy Davis wanted to know why Pearl had been forgotten when the Lutheran burying ground was moved in 1786.

As they searched historical documents, they found that in 1786 the city council of Albany decided to widen Pearl Street, which would require the Lutheran burying ground to be moved to a new cemetery a few blocks away. On May 18, 1786, James Food was offered "the Sum of two pounds twelve shillings and six pence, for taking up and Removing the Dead Bodies out of the Lutheran Burying ground. . . ; the said sum to be paid in Wheat."

For some reason, James Food overlooked a number of bodies. As the city widened Pearl Street throughout the 1790s, many skeletons were discovered in the area of the former burying ground. In 1791, Elbert Willett was paid by the City of Albany to construct a wooden box to bury some bones that had been left behind. In 1796, Edward Pangburn was compensated for "removing skeletons" from the area. In 1798, Lemual Hudson was reimbursed "for a box to contain skeletons." And in 1799, John Hyde was paid for carrying a "box of human bones" to the new burying ground, while Adam Todd was paid for "Burying a large Box of H. Bones."

Shortly after 1799, the widening of Pearl Street was finished, and no other skeletons were discovered at the site of the old Lutheran burying ground. But Pearl lay forgotten.

This watercolor painted by James Eights between 1840 and 1850 shows the corner of Pearl and State Streets in Albany. The privies might have been located in the backyards of the houses on the right.

The Privies of Pearl Street

Another interesting archaeological discovery under Pearl Street were two barrel privies (or outhouses), located not far from the burying ground. Probably built before 1780, the privies had two parts: an aboveground outhouse and a belowground barrel, made from white oak, which held the waste. The privies had most likely been located in the backyards of two residences near the northeast corner of Pearl and State Streets.

To determine what the people of the late 1700s were eating, archaeologists scooped out samples of the soil and analyzed them. They collected all the seeds from the samples and sorted them. Those in the highest numbers were raspberry, strawberry, bristly sarsaparilla, and grape. To find out how healthy the people of Albany were, they looked for signs of parasite eggs preserved in the soil. Poor sanitary conditions, common in colonial times, meant that people would become infected with worms. The archaeologists found eggs from whipworm, giant roundworm, and the thorn-headed worm, among others.

Many other colonial privies had been found in Albany during excavations over the years; they, too, had been analyzed the same way. When archaeologists compared the number of parasite eggs in all of the privies, they found that the two barrel privies on Pearl Street had far fewer eggs than the others. This meant that most residents of Pearl Street who used these privies were healthier than people in other parts of Albany. This was not because they practiced better sanitation. Instead, they had fewer parasites because, as wealthy Albanians, they were able to pay for medicine to help control their intestinal infections.

family had a cow, fed in a common pasture at the end of the town. In the evening they returned all together . . . along the wide and grassy street, to be milked at their master's door." Another visitor to Pearl's Albany might also have noticed (and smelled) one thing before all others: drainage ditches that ran down the dirt streets. In 1721 city leaders passed an ordinance that required citizens to "ditch and drain ye water to give it passage." This meant that human waste was deposited in the ditches. It is no wonder that a tourist in 1760 described Albany's streets as "the Dirtiest I ever Saw."

The wealthiest people in town lived near the Lutheran burying ground, and Pearl's skeleton revealed that she had most likely been the servant of a wealthy family. A wealthy woman with domestic servants in colonial Albany might have begun her morning by reading Scripture before breakfast, organizing her family's activities for the day, then retiring "to read in her closet . . . till about eleven." She could have eaten a late lunch, then entertained friends and other guests during the afternoon, reading and knitting during lulls in company. Pearl's skeleton, though, showed that she had performed hard labor throughout her life, as a result of very demanding duties.

But her bones could tell bioarchaeologists little about who she was. Was she single or married? Did she have a family? Had she been born in the colony, or had she emigrated there from a European country? And, the archaeologist Nancy Davis wondered, "while living in Albany, did she have any happiness?" After all, Davis knew that "she was probably in a lot of pain most of the time."

Scientists at the museum had one more question that they hoped could be answered: What did Pearl look like when she was alive? Because her skull was so well preserved, the sculptor Gay Malin was asked to reconstruct Pearl's face. Before she could begin, the archaeologist Andrea Lain of the New York State Museum first had to reassemble her skull, since it had been broken into pieces by the backhoe. Once that was done, Malin was ready to recreate her face.

First, Malin studied a forensic report on the woman, which

The anthropologist Andrea Lain painstakingly reassembles Pearl's skull so that a mold of it can be created.

The sculptor Gay Malin and the archeologist Chuck Fisher (right) of the New York State Museum inspect Pearl's skull before it was reconstructed.

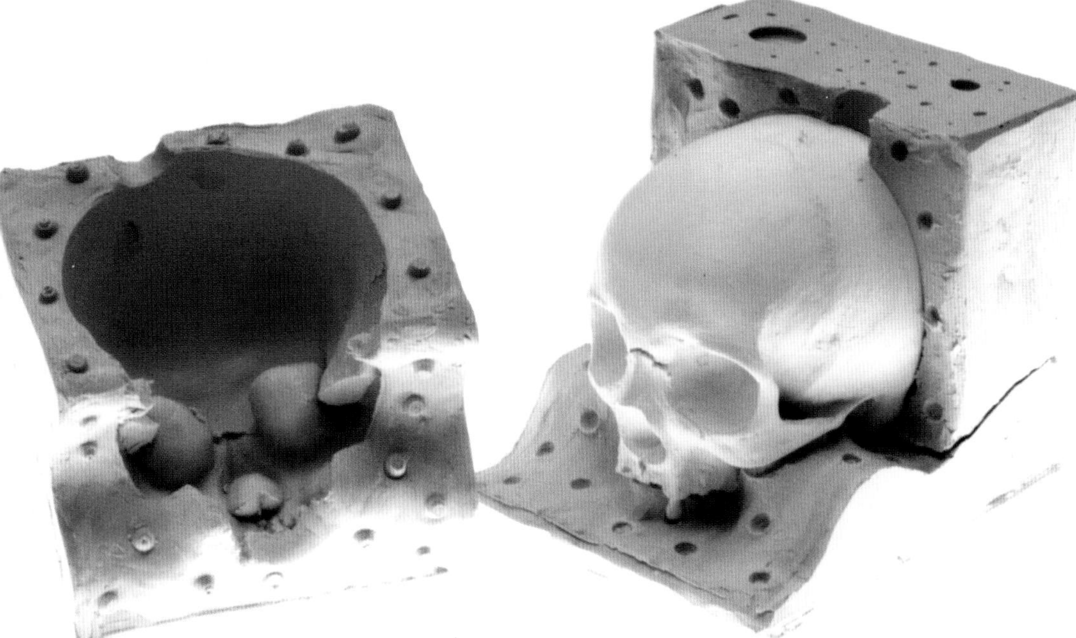

This mold was used to create a urethane replica of Pearl's original skull.

included her age, height, and illnesses visible from her skeleton. Because Pearl had lost so many teeth and had dental abscesses, Malin had to consider how these problems would have affected the look and shape of Pearl's face.

Then Malin made a mold of the skull and created a urethane (or plastic) replica of the original skull from the mold. Next, she placed tissue-depth markers onto the replica skull to indicate how deep the skin and tissues would be. To make the face as true to life and as accurate as possible, she consulted different scientific guides for average facial depths of a woman of Pearl's age and ancestry. Next she sculpted the facial-muscle groups onto the skull, then covered them and the rest of the skull with clay to simulate skin. Once the face was complete, Malin made another mold of her clay sculpture and filled it with a resin material to produce a final cast of Pearl. Then she airbrushed the face with Caucasian skin–toned paint and, after consulting with historians, added a historically correct hairstyle and cap.

The reconstruction process took almost three weeks. When it was completed, a forgotten, nameless woman from 1742 was suddenly facing museum workers and would soon appear in public. In 1998, some 256 years after Pearl died, a recreation of her face was put on display in a special exhibit about colonial Albany.

But her story wasn't over. On May 15, 1999, her remains were reburied along with the other two burials discovered near her by members of the Albany First Lutheran Church—Pearl's church. The ceremony was planned so that the opening hymn at the service was one that might have been sung during her lifetime.

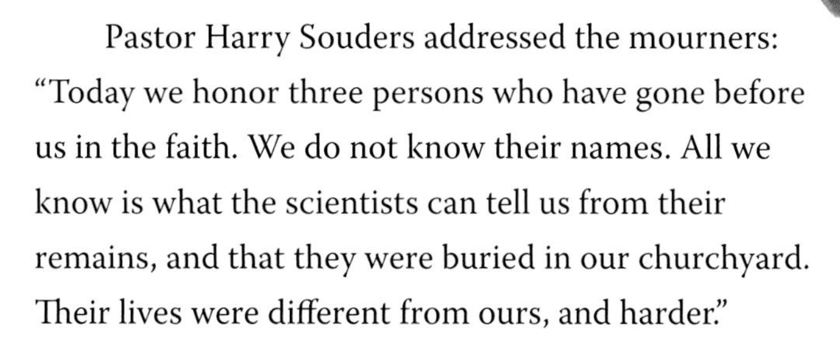

Pastor Harry Souders addressed the mourners: "Today we honor three persons who have gone before us in the faith. We do not know their names. All we know is what the scientists can tell us from their remains, and that they were buried in our churchyard. Their lives were different from ours, and harder."

After the morning service, the attendees went back to the First Lutheran Church, where they ate a lunch that might have been served at a funeral in the seventeenth century: ham, cheese, and rolls.

Pearl's face was reconstructed over a period of three weeks by Gay Malin.

The house at Schuyler Flatts was originally built around 1668. After a fire destroyed the roof and interior in 1759, the house was rebuilt. This photograph, taken about 1895, shows how the house looked at the time.

CHAPTER 6

The FORGOTTEN BURYING GROUND at Schuyler Flatts

CIRCA

1750–1790

Some grew up to work until they died. Others, though, were stricken with disease and died as infants or young children. Old or young, they had only first names, and after they were dead, no one kept a record of them or their location in the burying ground. Soon, all signs of their graves disappeared. When they were accidentally discovered hundreds of years later, a sad, hidden side of Schuyler Flatts became known.

In 1672, Philip Pieterse Schuyler, one of the first settlers of the Dutch colony of New Netherlands, purchased twenty-three acres, called the Flatts, along the Hudson River, four miles north of what would become Albany, New York. On the land was a large house that became the family home, from which he would oversee the activities of his farming estate.

As time passed, the Schuyler family prospered and grew into nine influential households in the Albany area. Philip's son Pieter, for example, became the first mayor of Albany in 1686, and two other Schuylers were mayors in the early 1700s. The Revolutionary War general Philip Schuyler spent time at the Flatts when he was a child.

For generations, the property at Schuyler Flatts was passed from one family member to another. In the 1800s, however, parts of the estate were sold off, and by 1929, the Schuylers were no longer the owners. The house was eventually abandoned and became a teenagers' hangout, before it burned to the ground under suspicious circumstances in 1962.

During its heyday, the estate at Schuyler Flatts was an important gathering place. Some early Dutch immigrants whose passage to New Netherlands was paid by others

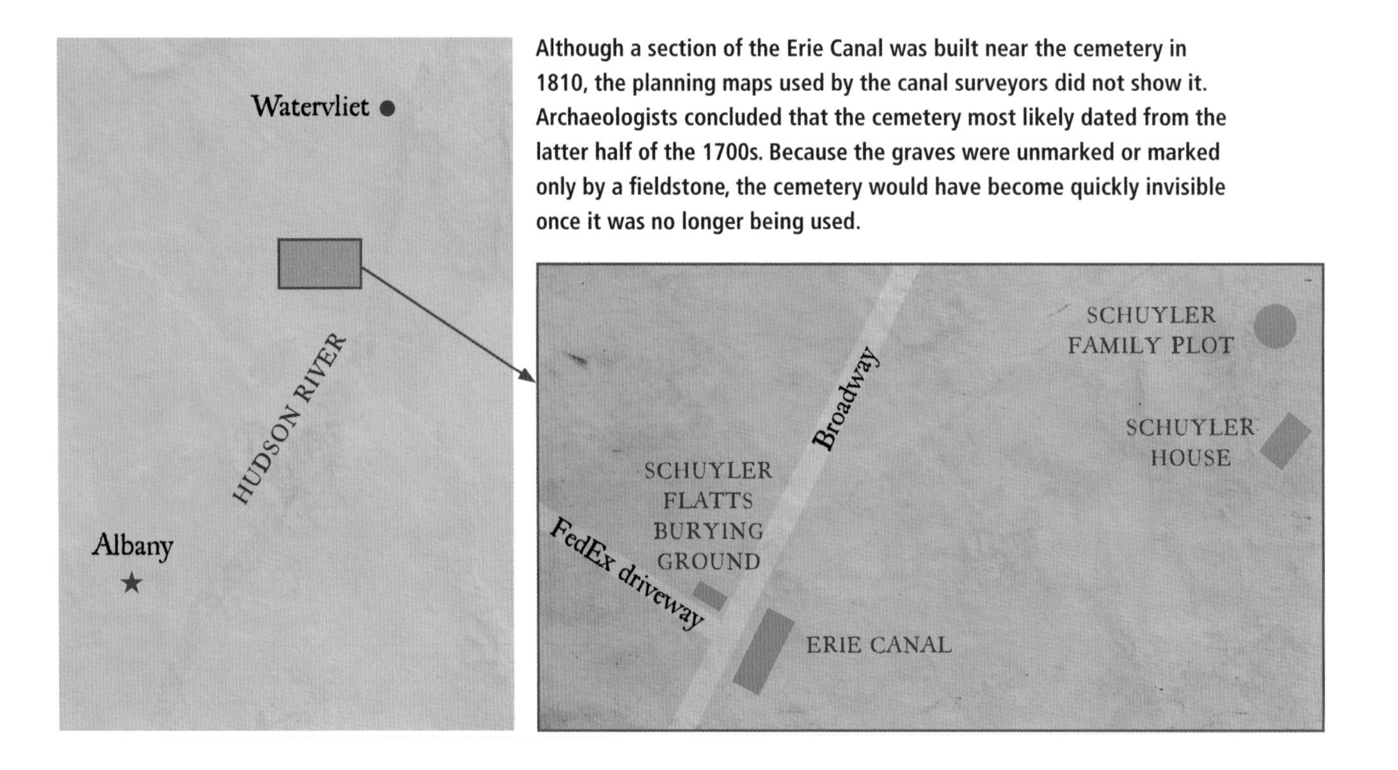

Although a section of the Erie Canal was built near the cemetery in 1810, the planning maps used by the canal surveyors did not show it. Archaeologists concluded that the cemetery most likely dated from the latter half of the 1700s. Because the graves were unmarked or marked only by a fieldstone, the cemetery would have become quickly invisible once it was no longer being used.

were required to work for a period (that is, they were indentured) at the Flatts. Native Americans traded furs with the Schuylers at the Flatts in the late 1600s. Wounded British soldiers were treated in a temporary hospital there after the 1758 Battle of Ticonderoga during the French and Indian War.

The original house at Schuyler Flatts was a large two-story building with one reception room, many bedrooms for the family and visitors, and an eating parlor with a kitchen beneath to help keep it warm in winter. Not far away, still on the estate, the Schuylers also maintained a cemetery, where generation after generation of family members were buried.

But the estate at Schuyler Flatts also had another cemetery, unmarked on any map, that would one day reveal another side of life there.

The area of darker soil indicated a burial shaft, in this case of a three-to-nine-month-old child.

The first sign of this long-lost cemetery was unexpectedly unearthed more than two hundred years after the cemetery was last used. As construction workers dug a new sewer line on June 3, 2005, they discovered two skeletons buried in coffins near a driveway for a Federal Express facility. Work stopped immediately, and construction supervisors called local and state police. When the police saw that the remains had most likely been buried in an old cemetery, archaeologists were summoned to photograph them, preserve them temporarily, and determine whether there were more graves in the construction zone. If so, they would need to excavate them before work could resume.

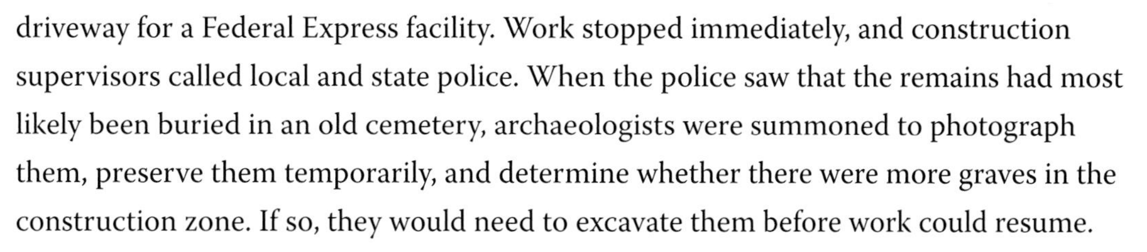

Over the next few days workers removed the topsoil, while archaeologists observed any variations in the color of the underlying earth. Rectangular shapes of darker soil indicated that a burial shaft for a grave had been dug. In all, they discovered thirteen people (six adults, two children, and five infants) in the two-row, unmarked cemetery. Each person had been wrapped in a cloth shroud and placed in a simple white pine coffin. Although the fabric had disintegrated and the coffin wood had rotted, archaeologists

Workers found the first burial off a major highway north of Albany, near the entrance to a FedEx facility.

As excavation of the cemetery continued, archaeologists placed flags to mark the presence of a burial.

were able to find pieces of cloth and wood, handmade iron coffin nails, and small brass straight pins that had fastened the burial shrouds. Each item was collected and saved.

As they excavated the graves, archaeologists scraped and brushed away the dirt to reveal the skeletal remains. Each skeleton was then examined by the anthropologist Erin Klinge, who attempted to determine the person's age, gender, any visible diseases, and ancestry. The children's skeletons had crumbled to bits and could not give much information, but the sturdier, adult skeletons would be able to tell stories about the person's life. Each of their bones was wrapped in acid-free tissue paper and bags and sent to the New York State Museum, where scientists and researchers would try to solve the mystery of who these people were and why they had been buried in the undocumented cemetery.

The first clue to the puzzle came from the coffin nails and the burial pins. By comparing them with others that had been found at similar sites, archaeologists were able to date the graves to sometime before 1820. A second clue emerged from Klinge's initial examination: The features of the adult skulls seemed to indicate African ancestry. A final clue

In the upper part of the burial shaft, archaeologists used trowels to scrape away the dirt (top). As they reached the burial, they switched to brushes to make sure that nothing was damaged (bottom).

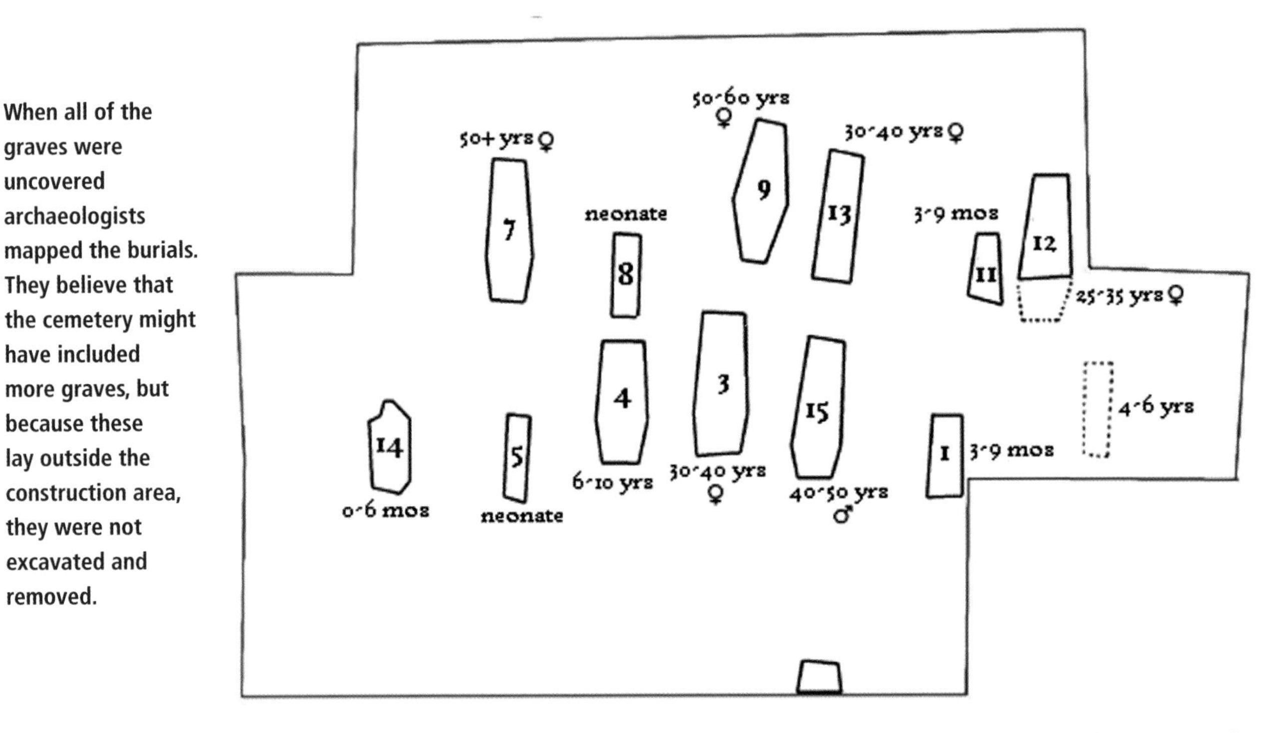

When all of the graves were uncovered archaeologists mapped the burials. They believe that the cemetery might have included more graves, but because these lay outside the construction area, they were not excavated and removed.

was found during a more detailed examination of the adult skeletons by the New York State Museum bioarchaeologists Vanessa Dale and Lisa Anderson; they saw indications in their bones that the people had performed repetitive hard labor throughout their lives. These three findings (burials before 1800, possible African ancestry, signs of hard labor) suggested that the graves probably contained the remains of enslaved people who had worked at Schuyler Flatts.

This possibility did not surprise local Albany historians. They knew that slavery had been not only an important part of the economy in Albany but an important factor in the Schuyler family's prosperity. In 1652, Albany had only a handful of slaves, almost all owned by the Dutch West India Company. Over the next twelve years, private citizens began to purchase slaves. After the British took possession of the colony in 1664, even more slaves were brought in to work on farming estates like the Schuylers'.

In 1711, after the deaths of Philip and Margarita Schuyler, who owned the Flatts at that time, an inventory of their property was drawn up. It listed among their property horses, cows, sheep, pigs, five men, and two women. Census records indicate that the Schuylers owned fourteen African slaves by the mid-1700s and many more by the end of the century. The Schuylers were not alone. In the 1790 census, 70 percent of all heads of household in the Albany region (808 out of 1,146) reported that they were slave-holding families. Then, in 1799, the state legislature passed the Gradual Emancipation

Inventory of Philip & Margarita Schuyler's Property, 1711

This is the inventory that was prepared in 1711, after the deaths of Philip and Margarita Schuyler, listing their possessions. The spellings are shown as they were originally written:

17 working horses
14 Cows
4 heffers
5 oxen
1 Bull
6 Calfs of a year Old

---

23 Sheep
17 young Lambs

---

5 Sows
1 Bore
14 or 15 Piggs

Account of negros and negro women
One negro Called Jacob
One ditto Called Charles
One ditto Called Peter
One ditto Called Thom
One ditto Called Anthony
One negro woman Called Mary
One ditto Called Bettie

Act, which called for the eventual freedom of slaves in New York, and the number of slaves gradually declined.

Anne Grant, a visitor from Scotland who lived with the widowed Margarita Schuyler at the Flatts for a number of years in the mid-1700s, later wrote a book about her stay. She noted that "the domestic friends of the family" (that is, their enslaved servants) lived in small bedrooms located in the attic. Among them, Grant recalled, were a carpenter, a shoemaker, and "a universal genius who made canoes, nets, and paddles; shod horses, . . . managed the fishing . . . , reared hemp and tobacco, and spun both; made cider, and tended wild horses . . . which it was his province to manage and to break."

Convinced that the life of the Schuylers' slaves was a good one, Grant commented:

> *I think I have never seen people so happy in servitude as the domestics. . . . They . . . were all born in the house, . . . baptized too, and shared the same religious instruction with the children of the family, and for the first years, there was little or no difference with regard to food or clothing between their children and those of their masters.*
>
> *When the negro-woman's child attained the age of three years, the first new year's day after, it was solemnly presented to a son or daughter, or other young relative of the family, who was of the same sex with the child so presented.*

The writer Anne Grant, who observed the enslaved workers at Schuyler Flatts, noted in her book that Schuyler slaves could be sold for "degeneracy." This 1895 painting by the artist Howard Pyle depicts a slave auction in New Amsterdam.

The child to whom the negro was given immediately presented it with some piece of money and a pair of shoes; and from that day the strongest attachment subsisted between the domestic and the destined owner.

She noted, though, that if a slave "showed symptoms of degeneracy, he was immediately expelled, or in other words most suitable to this case, sold." Even after Mrs. Schuyler died in 1784, the executors of her estate decided to sell one of her enslaved servants for unspecified reasons; an advertisement "offered 'a likely negro wench' for sale by auction at Lewis's tavern."

The discovery of the Schuyler Flatts cemetery gave New York State Museum researchers the opportunity to find out more about the lives of these enslaved people. Among other things, they wanted to study their ancestry by conducting a DNA study. To accomplish this, the molecular anthropologists at the State University of New York–Binghamton drilled one bone or tooth from each person to remove a powdery sample for testing. They then extracted mitochondrial DNA (mtDNA), which gives information about maternal ancestry. By comparing the mtDNA of the burials with that of various populations who have been tested around the world, the researchers found that all but

A Runaway Schuyler Slave

Peter S. Schuyler, who inherited the Flatts after his Aunt Margarita died in 1782, placed an advertisement in the local paper asking for the return of a runaway slave.

30 *Dollars Reward.*

RAN away from the subscriber . . . , a Negro Wench slave, named DEAUNA, aged about 20 years, very black, and well made, and may be called a handsome black. She took with her the following apparel: a homespun Petticoat and short Gown, a black silk Cloak, a purple calico Gown, and a light mixt coating Cloak with a large cape. She speaks English and Dutch well, and will tell a plausible story. 'Tis supposed she has gone to the eastward in a sleigh with a white man. The above reward will be paid to any person who will secure the said slave, or lodge her in any jail (gaol) in this state, by giving information to the subscriber.

PETER S. SCHUYLER
Feb. 3d, 1804

"at the cemetery, walnut grove plantation, south carolina, 1989" by Lucille Clifton

When the poet Lucille Clifton visited Walnut Grove Plantation in 1989, she was stunned to learn that the slaves who built the plantation were not mentioned on her tour. She wrote the following poem to help people "recognize that only half the truth was being told." Eventually, the owners of the plantation revised the tour to include all of the people who had lived and worked there.

among the rocks
at walnut grove
your silence drumming
in my bones,
tell me your names.
nobody mentioned slaves
and yet the curious tools
shine with your fingerprints.
nobody mentioned slaves
but somebody did this work
who had no guide, no stone,
who moulders under rock.
tell me your names,
tell me your bashful names
and i will testify.
the inventory lists ten slaves
but only men were
recognized.
among the rocks
at walnut grove
some of those honored dead
were dark
some of these slaves
were women
some of them did this
honored work.
tell me your names
foremothers, brothers,
tell me your dishonored
names.
here lies
here lies
here lies
here lies
hear

one adult had a mother, grandmother, or great-grandmother who had been born in Africa; three had links to west-central Africa, two to East Africa, and two to the island of Madagascar, off Africa's eastern coast. They were not related to one another, at least on their maternal side. The mtDNA results added even stronger evidence that almost all of the burials had been enslaved Africans who worked at Schuyler Flatts.

Next, researchers at the museum were anxious to put faces on these nameless, forgotten people. The artist Gay Malin reconstructed the faces of the adults in clay, but only two received final casts: the women known as Burials 9 and 3.

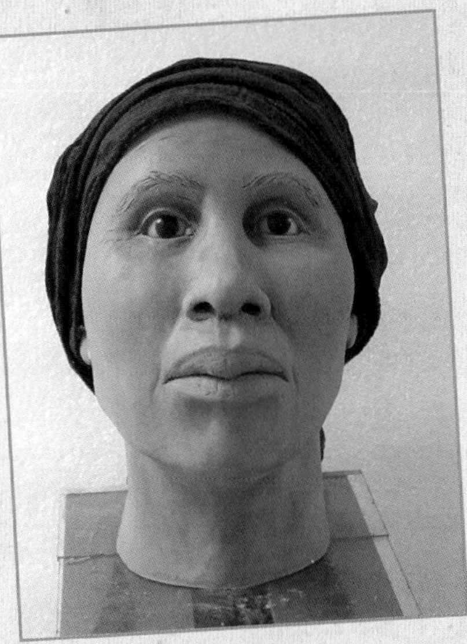

Burial 3
30-40 year old woman

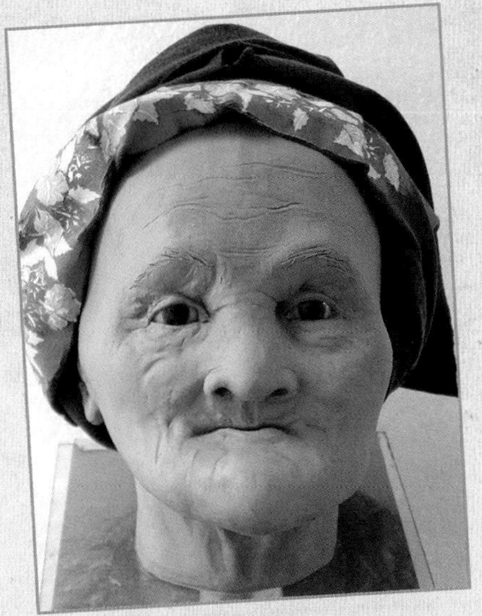

Burial 7
50+ year old woman

Burial 9
50-60 year old woman

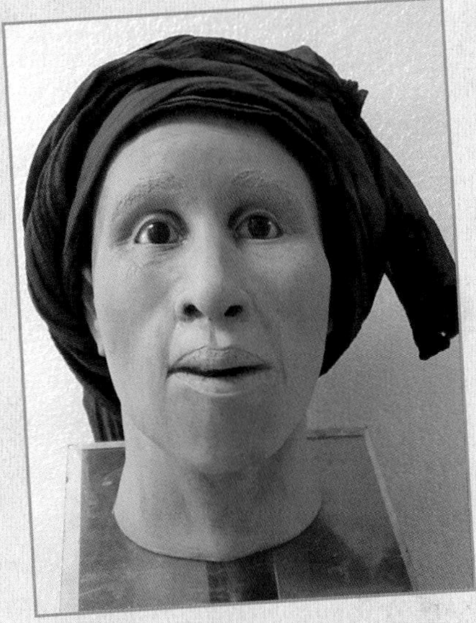

Burial 13
30-40 year old woman

1998 Burial
30-35 year old woman

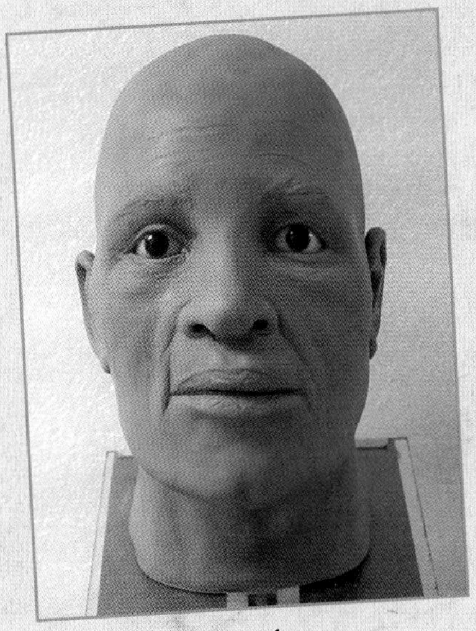

Burial 15
40-50 year old man

This poster, created by the museum, shows the faces of all six adults, as rendered by Gay Malin in clay. They are among the relatively few slave burials whose skeletons have been accidentally discovered.

Gay Malin was able to make final casts of only two burials. Burial 3 (left) had both Native American and African ancestry, according to bioarchaeologists. Burial 9 (right) had ancestors in Madagascar.

Burial 9. This five-foot-four-inch woman was approximately fifty-five years old when she died. Her mtDNA was traced to Madagascar, the profitable home of the slave trade in the late 1700s and early 1800s. Many Malagasy people (people from Madagascar) were captured by pirates and sold into slavery; they arrived in New York on slave ships, some owned by a wealthy New York family named Philips. The Schuylers knew the Philipses and may well have purchased Malagasay slaves from them.

The bones of Burial 9 told the bioarchaeologist Vanessa Dale that she was strong and hard-working, with well-developed muscles in her right shoulder and the large joints in the lower part of her body (her hips, knees, and ankles). But she had severe arthritis in her left hand, her toes, and her lower spine, where some vertebrae had fused together, probably due to heavy lifting. Dale also discovered that Burial 9's left arm was slightly shorter than her right and that for some reason the bone at the lower part of the skull had developed unevenly; this meant that she may have held her head to the left side. Finally, a dental exam showed that she had lost quite a few teeth during her lifetime and that the remaining ones were full of cavities and covered with plaque. Rounded grooves in her front teeth indicated that she had smoked a pipe for many years.

Burial 3. This approximately forty-year-old woman surprised the archaeologists. Through the features of her skull indicated that she was of African descent, her mtDNA told another story: A close female relative was Native American and possibly a Micmac Indian from the coastal regions of Maine or Canada. Dale and Anderson wondered if she had a father of African descent and if she, too, had been enslaved at Schuyler Flatts.

Her teeth were in poor condition, and she was missing many molars. Horizontal lines in her teeth, which showed that her tooth enamel had temporarily stopped forming at different points, revealed that she had poor nutrition or was quite ill when she was a child. Anthropologists could not find a cause of death revealed in her bones, but they did find signs of a well-healed fracture of the left wrist, mild arthritis in her major joints, and severe arthritis in her lower back.

The reconstructed faces of these two women will eventually be placed on display in the New York State Museum as part of an exhibit about the long-forgotten Schuyler Flatts burying ground and the enslaved people who were interred there.

Were the enslaved domestic workers, as Anne Grant wrote in 1808, "so happy in servitude"?

Their skeletons told a story of pain and unending work.

The Voice of Isabella Baumfree

Although the enslaved workers of Schuyler Flatts left no record of their lives, a few slaves who lived in New York State did manage to be recorded in history. One of them was a woman named Isabella Baumfree, who was born into slavery in 1797. Sold at the age of nine with a flock of sheep for one hundred dollars, Isabella was sold twice more by the time she was thirteen.

Two years after her birth, the New York State legislature passed an act that provided for the eventual freedom of all slaves. Isabella's owner, Mr. Dumont, told her that "he would give her 'free papers,' one year before she was legally free." When the time came, he told her that he had changed his mind. Because she had a diseased hand, he told her she hadn't worked hard enough to earn her freedom.

In a biography that she dictated later in her life, Isabella—who had changed her named to Sojourner Truth—told how she reacted to Mr. Dumont:

"Ah!" she says, with emphasis that cannot be written, "the slaveholders are TERRIBLE for promising to give you this or that, or such and such a privilege, if you will do thus and so; and when the time of fulfilment comes, and one claims the promise, they . . . recollect nothing of the kind: and you are . . . taunted with being a LIAR; or, at best, the slave is accused of not having performed his part or condition of the contract."

"Oh!" said she, "I have felt as if I could not live through the operation sometimes. Just think of us! so eager for our pleasures, and just foolish enough to keep feeding and feeding ourselves up with the idea that we should get what had been thus fairly promised; and when we think it is almost in our hands, find ourselves flatly denied! Just think! how could we bear it? Why, there was Charles Brodhead promised

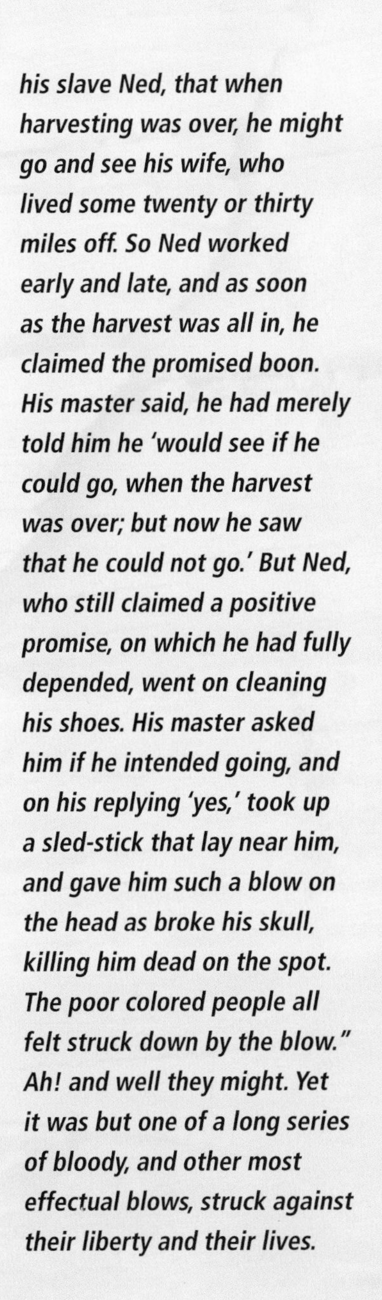
his slave Ned, that when harvesting was over, he might go and see his wife, who lived some twenty or thirty miles off. So Ned worked early and late, and as soon as the harvest was all in, he claimed the promised boon. His master said, he had merely told him he 'would see if he could go, when the harvest was over; but now he saw that he could not go.' But Ned, who still claimed a positive promise, on which he had fully depended, went on cleaning his shoes. His master asked him if he intended going, and on his replying 'yes,' took up a sled-stick that lay near him, and gave him such a blow on the head as broke his skull, killing him dead on the spot. The poor colored people all felt struck down by the blow." Ah! and well they might. Yet it was but one of a long series of bloody, and other most effectual blows, struck against their liberty and their lives.

Sojourner Truth's book, Narrative of Sojourner Truth: A Northern Slave, told of her life as a slave in Upstate New York.

She ran away from Mr. Dumont in 1826 and spent the better part of her life fighting against slavery and promoting women's rights.

The 1836 Battle of San Jacinto was depicted in this carefully researched painting by Henry Arthur McArdle, completed in 1895.

CHAPTER 7

A MEXICAN SOLDIER *from San Jacinto*

The soldier was killed in a brutal battle, his body left with hundreds of others to rot in a field. After a year, his skull was picked up and given to a collector, who catalogued it and placed it on a shelf. Eventually, it came to rest in a Pennsylvania museum. Many years later a researcher found the forgotten skull and made sure that the soldier's story was told.

During a trip along the Gulf coast of Texas in April 1837, the naturalist John James Audubon spent two weeks collecting various specimens that he could study and possibly illustrate in his books. He found a new species of rattlesnake, a large swordfish, a flower that he nicknamed the Texas daisy, and many species of ducks, wild turkeys, and other birds.

But the most unusual items that Audubon collected during his trip were four human skulls—the remains of Mexican soldiers who had been killed a year before at the Battle of San Jacinto.

One of the briefest battles and most brutal massacres on the continent of North America, the Battle of San Jacinto was the final land encounter in the Texas War for Independence from Mexico. In the late afternoon of April 21, 1836, some 900 Texan soldiers (that is, Americans living in the Mexican state of Tejas, or Texas, as they called it,

The Texas War for Independence

Colonel James Fannin was shot by a firing squad at the fort of La Bahía not long after most of his men were massacred by Mexican troops.

After Mexico gained independence from Spain in 1821, its government encouraged American citizens to move to its sparsely populated northern state named Coahuila y Tejas (Texas), where they became farmers and ranchers. They were allowed to buy land cheaply, if they agreed to become Mexican citizens and convert to the Catholic faith; neither requirement, however, was enforced. They were also allowed to bring their enslaved workers with them, which many of the emigrating white Americans found especially appealing.

By 1830, the American population of Coahuila y Tejas far outnumbered the Mexicans. Concerned that the United States might try to claim the northern state as its own, the Mexican government cracked down on the American settlers, passing a decree that discouraged any further emigration of Americans to Tejas. Angered by the new law, American residents held two conventions at which they requested

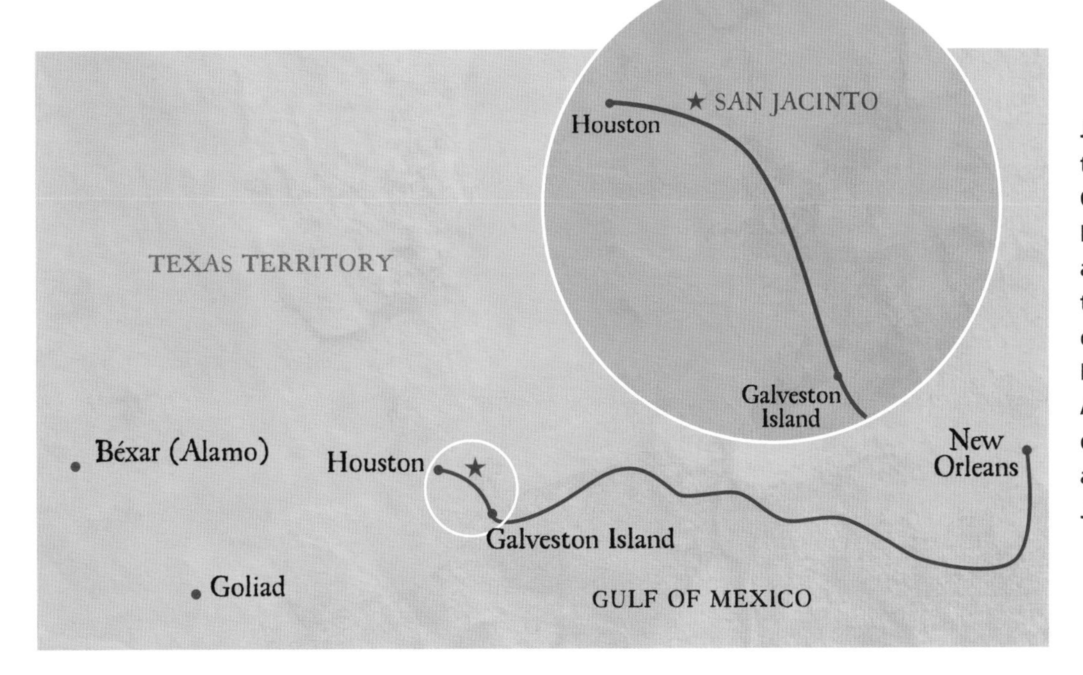

John James Audubon traveled from New Orleans to Galveston Island and Houston, a year after the final three land battles of the War for Texas Independence: the Alamo at San Antonio de Béxar, La Bahía at Goliad, and San Jacinto.

statehood for Tejas. But when Antonio López de Santa Anna became president in 1834, he took a hard stance against the Americans. The Texans revolted, and a war of independence began in October 1835.

Although the war lasted less than seven months, the hostility between the two sides was intense, especially in the final three land battles.

In the first of these, the Battle of the Alamo, Mexican troops under the command of President Santa Anna besieged the small mission near the town of San Antonio de Béxar for thirteen days beginning February 23, 1836. On the morning of March 6, Santa Anna ordered his men to storm the Alamo. All of the approximately two hundred Texan defenders died in the final assault, their bodies later burned near a grove of trees.

Less than two weeks later, at the Battle of Coleta Creek, the Texans were badly outnumbered. Their commander, Colonel James Fannin, ordered his 342 men to surrender, figuring that they would be traded for Mexican prisoners in a short time. Instead, they were escorted to La Bahía, an old Spanish fort near Goliad. Then Santa Anna ordered their execution.

On March 27, 1836, a hot Palm Sunday morning, Fannin's men, unaware of Santa Anna's order, were marched from the fort toward the San Antonio River, where their guards opened fire at close range. Only twenty-eight Texans managed to escape; others who tried to run were chased down by soldiers on horseback and killed. Colonel Fannin himself, unable to walk because of a wounded leg, was executed in front of a firing squad. Then the bodies of Fannin and most of his men were placed in a shallow trench and burned.

As the news of the two massacres at the Alamo and La Bahía spread, Texans grew more incensed with Santa Anna's brutality. So when the brief Battle of San Jacinto ended, Texan soldiers took brutal revenge.

The Texan Soldiers

Very few of the soldiers fighting for Texas independence had been born there. According to the historian Paul D. Lack, 76 percent of the Texan troops had emigrated to the Texas territory from southern states; the rest came from northern states and from foreign countries. Most had arrived in Texas not long before—either in 1834 or early 1835.

The mostly white Texan force included five free blacks and twenty-nine Tejano soldiers (Mexicans who wanted to break away from Mexico). Captain Juan N. Seguín led a twenty-four-man company of Tejanos, all but one born in the Texas territory. A well-respected soldier, Seguín was responsible for burying the ashes of the dead from the Alamo. He was elected to the Texas Senate and later became mayor of San Antonio. Five other Tejanos (Major Lorenzo de Zavala Jr., Peter Lopez, Martin Flores, Antonio Treviño, and José Molino) were members of other companies. Major Zavala, who reported directly to Sam Houston, the commander of the Texans, was instrumental in translating captured letters intended for the enemy commander, Santa Anna.

fighting for independence from Mexico) surprised and overwhelmed a larger, freshly reinforced army of 1,250 Mexican soldiers.

In eighteen minutes the battle was over. And then the massacre began.

As Mexican soldiers fled the battlefield, Texan soldiers swarmed after them. Even when the Mexicans held up white flags of surrender, the Texan soldiers, remembering the battles at the Alamo and La Bahía in which Texas soldiers had been killed and their bodies burned, used their rifles to shoot or club the Mexican soldiers to death.

William S. Taylor, a member of the Texas cavalry, described what happened as he chased the Mexican soldiers: "While pursuing the Mexicans on the road . . . we overtook numbers . . . and . . . felt compelled to kill them, and did so, though on their knees crying for quarter, and saying, 'Me no Alamo—me no la Bahia,' meaning that they were not in either of those horrible massacres. As there were but some fifteen or eighteen of us, and some sixty of the Mexicans we were pursuing . . . , we saw it was impossible for us to take prisoners."

In all, about six hundred Mexican soldiers were killed that day, while the rest were taken prisoner. Only nine Texans died from their wounds in the battle; they were buried near the army camp at Buffalo Bayou, but the dead Mexican soldiers were left where they lay.

No one can explain why the Mexican dead were never buried. Some place the blame on the Texans, who did not have enough men or enough interest to bury the fallen soldiers. Others say that the Mexican president and army commander Antonio López de

Santa Anna, who was captured after the battle, showed no concern about the burial of his own men. Their bodies lay on the battlefield as buzzards, coyotes, and even cows ate the flesh from the remains. Some witnesses also observed a dentist from the United States extracting teeth from the dead soldiers for use in his practice.

A year later Audubon visited the battleground at San Jacinto and mentioned it briefly in his journal. He observed "the scattered remains of numerous individuals destroyed in that bloody fray." Then he gathered four skulls, not as souvenirs but as a gift for a Philadelphia doctor who wanted to amass a worldwide crania (skull) collection.

From 1832 to 1851, Dr. Samuel George Morton acquired 867 skulls with the help of a network of 138 friends and associates, such as Audubon, who sent him skulls when they came across—or stole—them. For example, a Cuban doctor sent Morton the skulls of "fifty-five Africans—including girls and boys as young as twelve—who had died as slaves on a sugar plantation outside Havana." Another collector sent him the skulls of Chinese pirates executed by hanging. Audubon himself sent Morton the four skulls from San Jacinto. When they were catalogued, they

Today a granite marker indicates the location of the massacre of Mexican soldiers on the San Jacinto Battleground State Historic Site.

The four skulls collected by John James Audubon in 1837 were given to Samuel George Morton for his crania collection. They were catalogued and numbered 555 through 558. Audubon also collected a fifth skull, but for unknown reasons, it was labeled number 690 when it was added to Morton's collection.

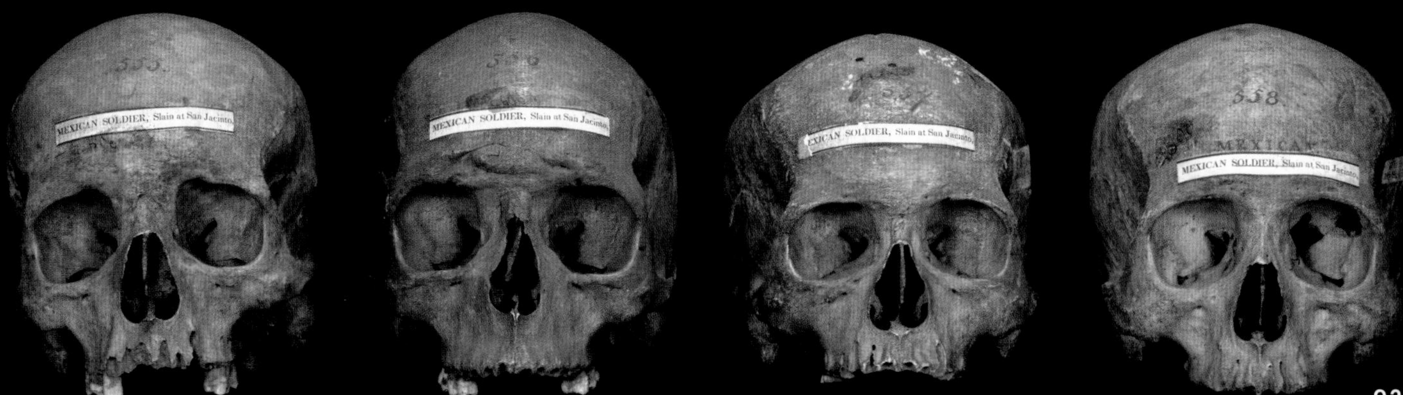

The skulls of the four Mexican soldiers from the San Jacinto battleground are stored with the rest of the Morton collection at the University of Pennsylvania Museum of Archaeology and Anthropology.

were given the numbers 555 through 558.

After Morton's death, his skulls were displayed at the Academy of Natural Sciences in Philadelphia, where even more skulls were added. Sometimes certain skulls were loaned to other exhibits, such as in 1892 when "the Academy sent 44 of the Native American crania to Spain for the 400th anniversary of Columbus's discovery of the New World." Around 1965 the collection was transferred to the University of Pennsylvania Museum of Archaeology and Anthropology. By then, few people knew of the collection and no one remembered that it included at least four skulls from the battleground at San Jacinto.

All that would change in January 2009 when Jeff Dunn—a Dallas lawyer, a history buff, and cofounder of the San Jacinto Battleground Conservancy—was researching the battle on the Internet. He came across a mention of the San Jacinto skulls in Morton's catalogue of human crania. In a short time, Dunn was able to locate the skulls at the University of Pennsylvania. Then the San Jacinto Battleground Conservancy contacted the Smithsonian Institution to ask if anthropologists would examine the skulls to learn more about these four Mexican soldiers.

In January 2010 a team of researchers from the Smithsonian Institution, headed by the anthropologist Douglas Owsley, went to Philadelphia to study the skulls. Owsley found that the four soldiers ranged in age from about thirty to forty when they were killed. Two of the men (Skulls 557 and 558) died from fatal gunshot wounds to the head. Because of the angle of the bullet wounds, researchers surmised that the two men were probably on their knees attempting to surrender when they were shot from above. The skulls of the other two men (Skulls 555 and 556) did not offer any clues to their deaths during the battle, but they did reveal that the men had been previously injured.

This replica of Skull 558 shows the path of the fatal gunshot wound that killed this Mexican soldier at San Jacinto. Because the bullet entered from above, scientists have concluded that he may have been on his knees attempting to surrender.

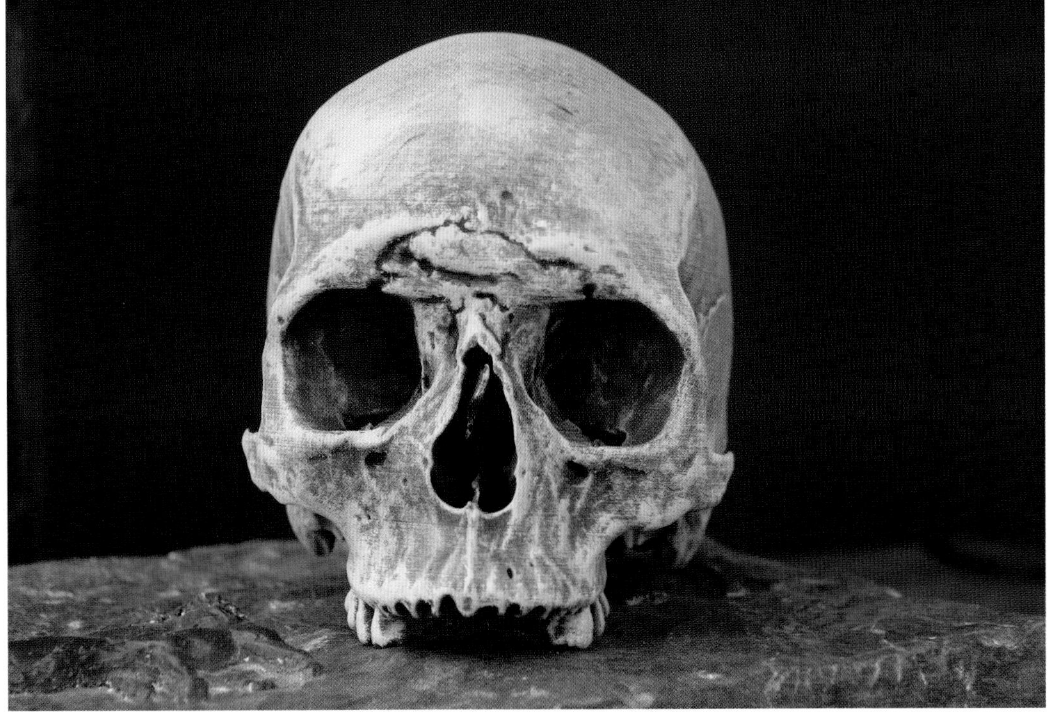

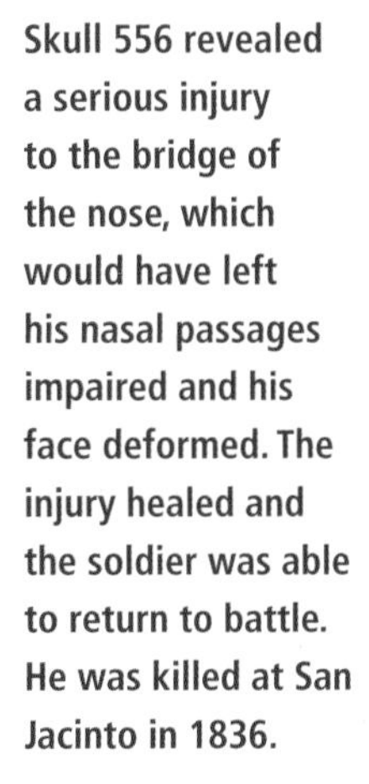

Skull 556 revealed a serious injury to the bridge of the nose, which would have left his nasal passages impaired and his face deformed. The injury healed and the soldier was able to return to battle. He was killed at San Jacinto in 1836.

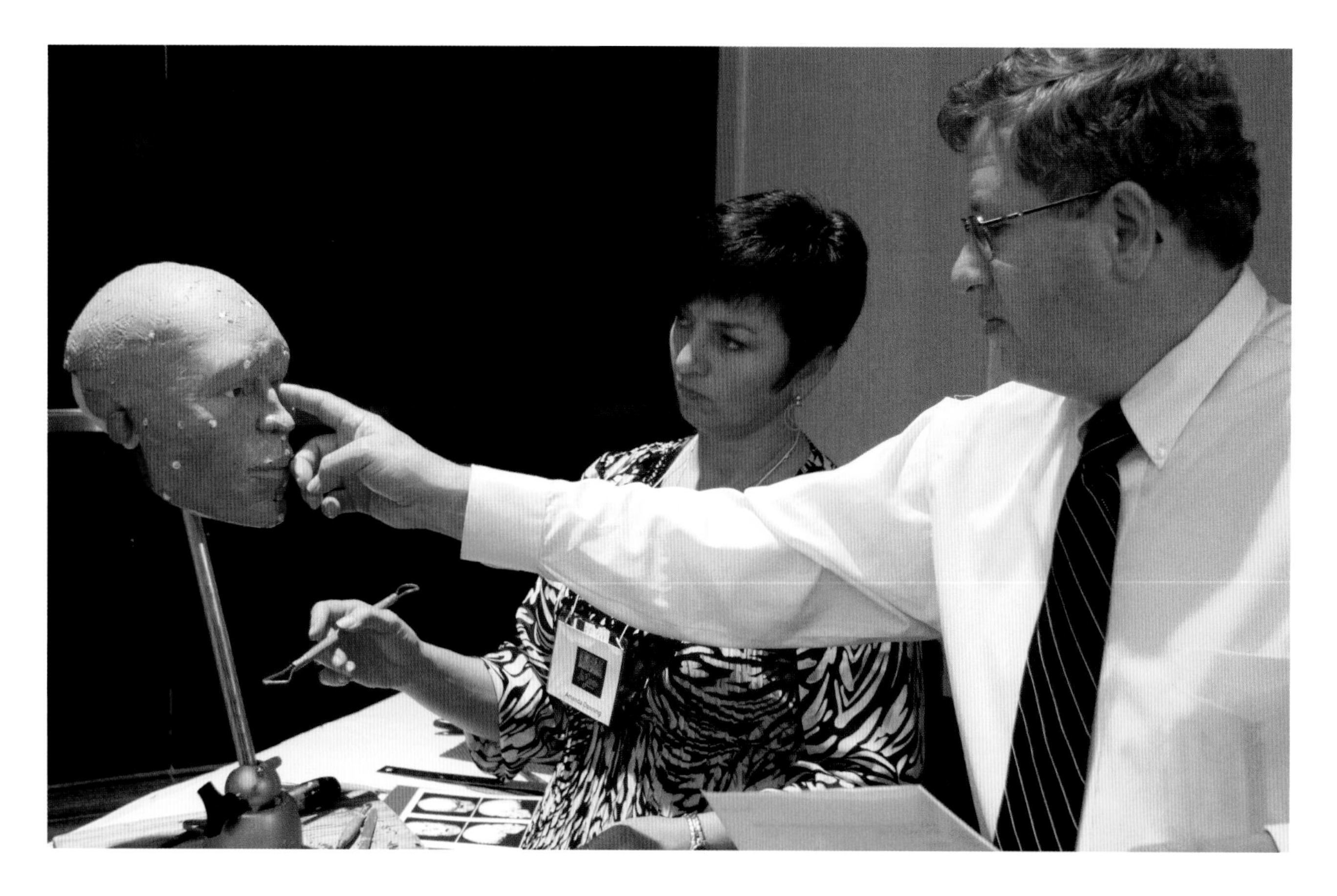

The anthropologist Douglas Owsley of the Smithsonian Institution consults with the sculptor Amanda Danning as she reconstructs the face of the Mexican soldier.

Skull 555 had three circular injuries on the back right side. Dr. Morton had concluded—and Owsley agreed—that the man had been wounded by buckshot, fired from a great enough distance that the skull was not penetrated, only dented.

The injury to Skull 556, though, was much more life-threatening. About a year before the Battle of San Jacinto, the man had been hit squarely in the face, probably by a rifle butt. In his report, Owsley wrote that the "nose and midface were severely damaged. Breathing through the nasal chamber was significantly impaired." Although the wounds of both men had healed, the man with Skull 556 would have been disfigured and unable to breathe normally. Still, both men returned to combat. Were they killed during the battle or during its tragic aftermath? There was no way to determine this.

To honor the Mexican soldiers, the San Jacinto Battleground Conservancy asked the artist Amanda Danning to reconstruct the faces of the soldiers. Skull 556 was

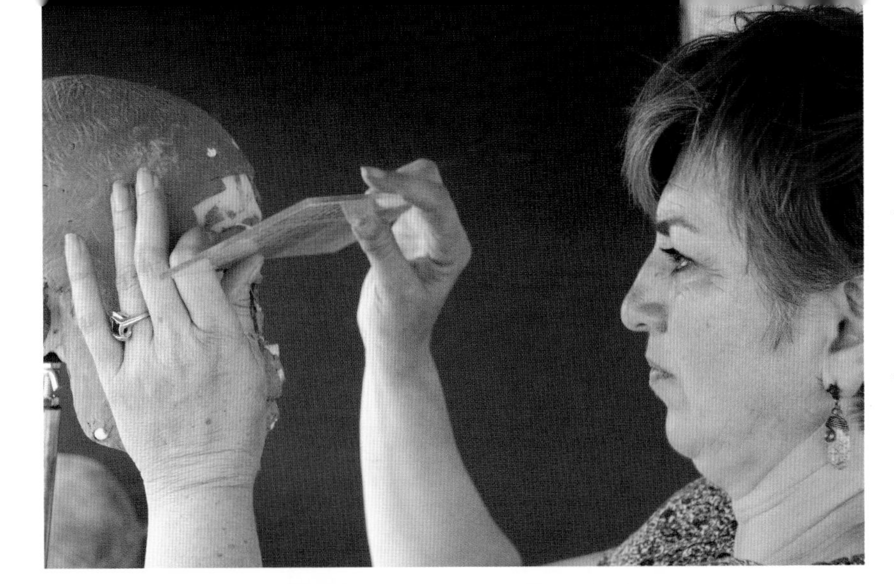

Making a reconstruction is a painstaking process that involves precise measuring. Here Amanda Danning works on a reconstruction of the Mexican soldier's face as it would have appeared after a severe facial injury, which he received about a year before his death at San Jacinto.

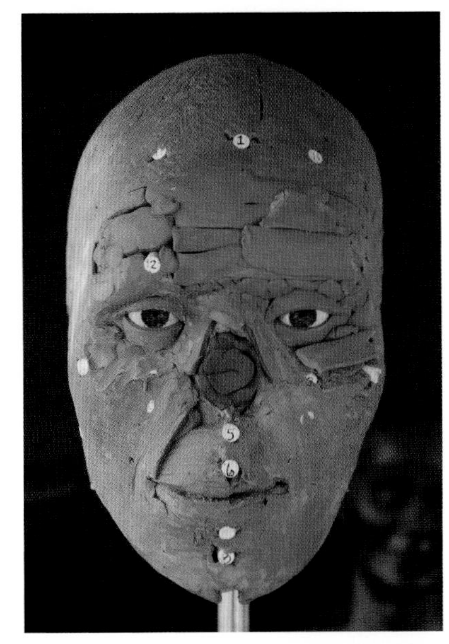

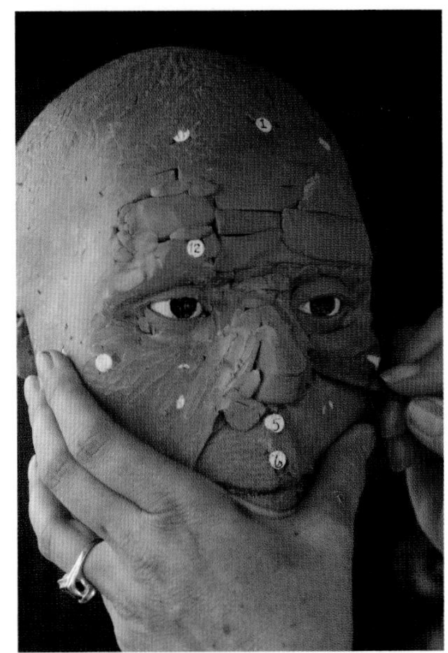

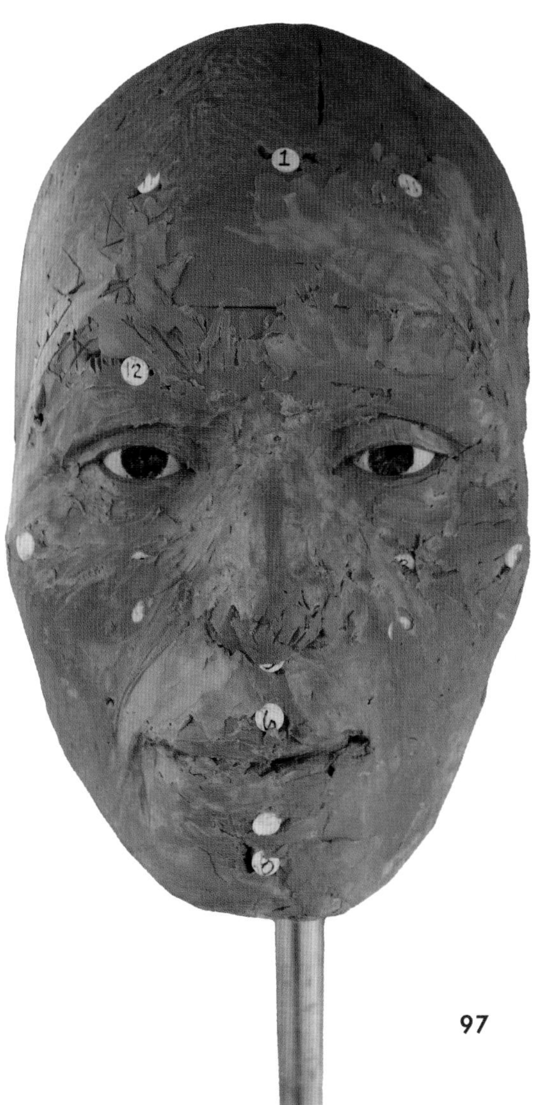

The two faces of the Mexican soldier known as Skull 556 were placed on display at the Sam Houston Memorial Museum in Huntsville, Texas.

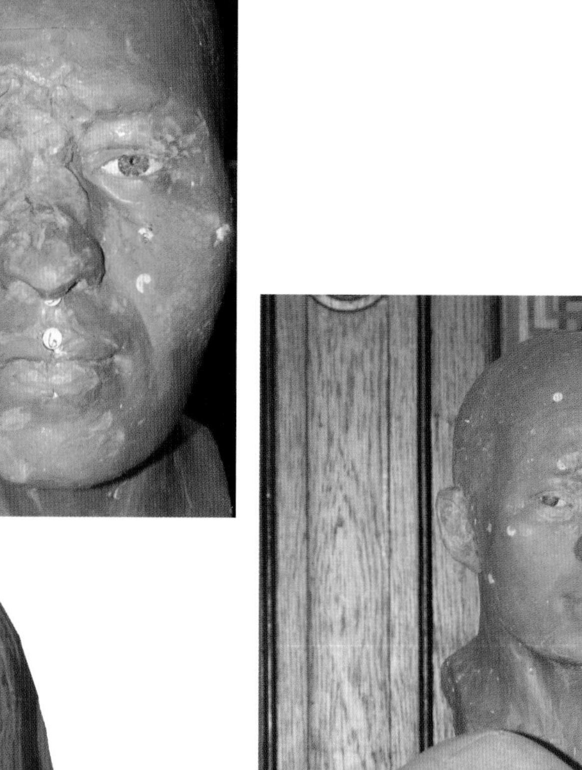

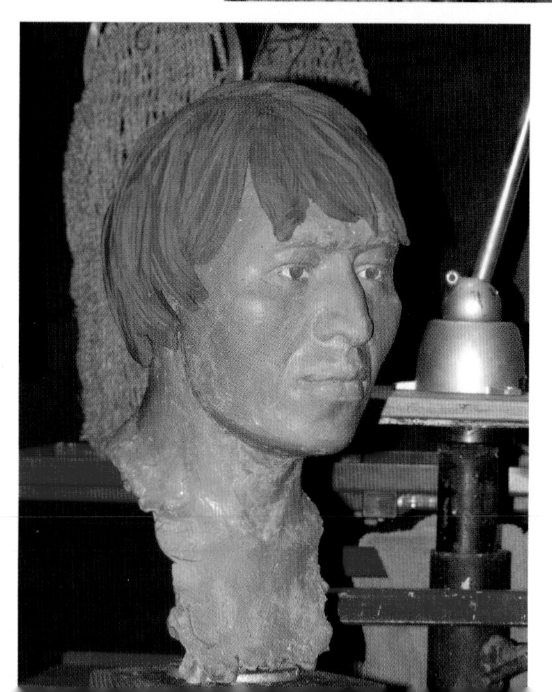

selected first, then CT-scanned so that a replica could be made. By reconstructing his face, Danning hoped to show that "not only do you get to look at the face of someone who fought at San Jacinto, probably fought at the Alamo and certainly fought at some other type of battle, you're also going to get to see how much tougher people were back then."

Then Danning recreated his face—in two versions. First, she built his face to appear as it would have without the injury. Next, she reconstructed it exactly as it was when he died—with the healed damage done by the rifle butt.

Then the two faces of the Mexican soldier who had been silenced in war were able to communicate again to those who saw him on exhibit at various Texas museums. The faces revealed the pain of his facial injury, his strength in returning to battle after the injury, and his determination and bravery in fighting for his country, no matter what the cost.

The Dallas lawyer and amateur historian Jeff Dunn tracked down the San Jacinto skulls. Here he stands next to a monument honoring the Texas soldiers who died at the Battle of San Jacinto.

The Albany County Almshouse was built in 1826 to provide shelter and food for the poor and sick of Albany, New York.

CHAPTER 8

The People of the ALMSHOUSE CEMETERY

CIRCA

1826–1926

They were the poorest people in town when they were buried in the almshouse cemetery. The oldest of them died in the almshouse hospital or dormitory, the youngest in the nursery at birth. Still others died in the nearby penitentiary or in the river. And when the almshouse eventually closed, its cemetery was forgotten until new buildings needed to be built. Then the graves had to be uncovered, and the secrets of the cemetery were revealed.

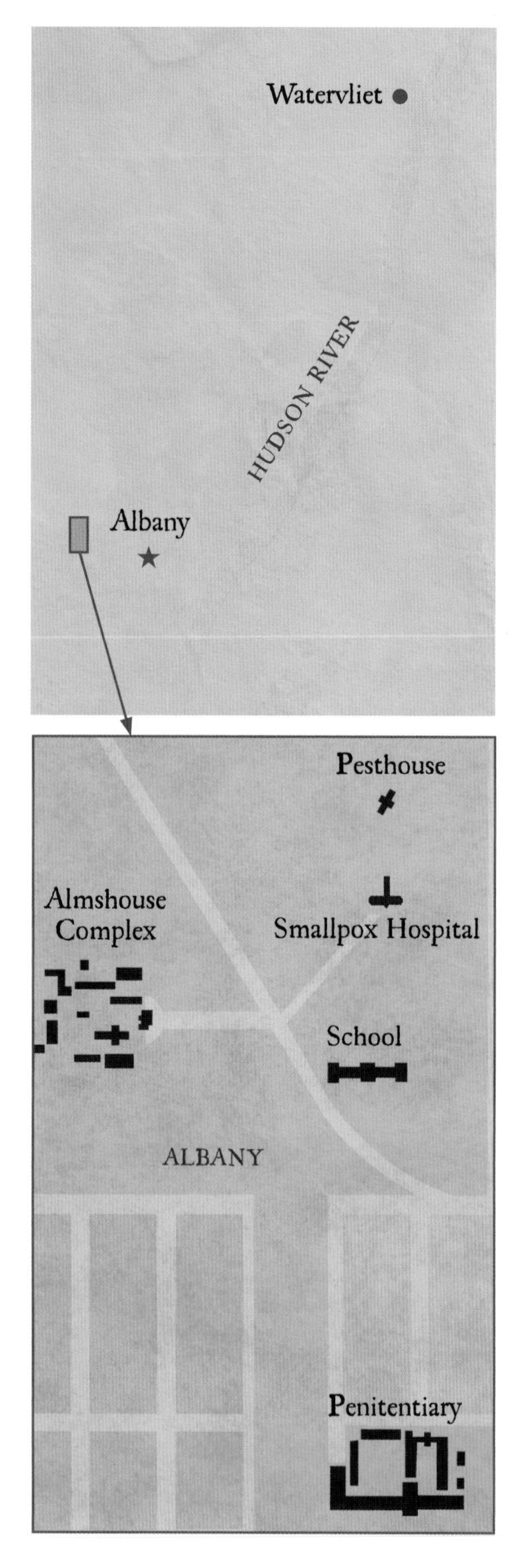

The Albany County Almshouse was located on a 116-acre working farm, which included a "pesthouse," a school for "vagrant children," and a smallpox hospital. Nearby was the Albany Medical College and a penitentiary.

The 1999 archaeology report was clear: Developers of an $80 million medical-research facility in Albany, New York, could expect to find up to 225 bodies when construction began. The building site had once been part of a 116-acre farm that housed the Albany County Almshouse (sometimes called the poorhouse).

Once a common institution in many towns, the almshouse was intended to provide a short-term home for people who were too poor or too sick to care for themselves. After a short stay, residents were expected to leave and take over their support. Many almshouse residents were immigrants, especially from Ireland. Trying to escape from the Great Famine between 1845 and 1852, Irish immigrants had heard that there were jobs in Albany. However, because many were sick when they arrived and unable to work, they were admitted to the almshouse and hospitals until they were well again and could earn a living.

Often, though, older people who could no longer live alone were also admitted. For example, Margaret Coffee emigrated to the United States from Ireland when she was thirty. She worked for eighteen years as a seamstress, until her eyesight began to fail. When she applied for admission to the Albany County Almshouse around 1868, the clerk wrote, "This woman is honest, sober, and industrious. She supported herself for a number of years after her husband's death. Being afflicted with sore eyes, she was compelled to seek admission here."

The Albany almshouse opened in 1826 and closed in 1926. During its lifetime, the complex included separate men's and women's dormitories, a kitchen and dining hall, a chapel, a hospital, and a "lunatic" asylum. Also on the farm were a "pesthouse" for people with contagious diseases such as tuberculosis, a vocational school for vagrant children, a smallpox hospital, and a cemetery.

The cemetery had been used for one hundred years and held the graves not only of people who died in the almshouse but of others who died at a nearby penitentiary and orphanage. It also served as a potter's field for the City of Albany—that is, as a burial place for people who could not afford to pay for a burial or for people who were unidentified or unclaimed by relatives after they died.

When the almshouse was finally closed, the cemetery was not relocated. Its unmarked graves were forgotten as the decades passed. According to cemetery records from 1880 to 1926, almost twenty-five hundred people were known to have been buried there. But there were no burial records before 1880. Researchers guessed that a total of five thousand people, or perhaps more, had been interred in the cemetery during its one-hundred-year lifetime.

The medical-facility developers, perhaps relieved that only 225 burials

Residents of an Indiana poorhouse were photographed eating their noon meal in 1949. The meals provided by the Albany almshouse were probably smaller, according to the menu shown below.

One Day of Almshouse Meals

In 1834 the following daily menu plan was proposed for the Albany almshouse.

ALBANY ALMSHOUSE

BREAKFAST: bohea [inexpensive black] tea sweetened with molasses and bread thinly spread with butter before put on the table.

DINNER [LUNCH]: beef soup and bread every day except Tuesday and Friday, on which days codfish and potatoes with bread.

SUPPER: mush sweetened with molasses, of which two spoonsfull allowed each person.

Since the excavation of the cemetery was begun in the middle of winter, a large tent was erected to protect the workers and keep them warm.

would need to be relocated, agreed to hire a team of archaeologists to excavate the burials and anthropologists to study the human remains at the site. Their only condition was that the scientists would have just one month from the time a grave was discovered to excavate and study the skeleton before they had to give them to a local funeral director for reburial at another Albany cemetery. This time limit, developers hoped, would prevent any further delays to the building project. The scientists accepted this condition, since they were intrigued by the chance to study the remains of a group of people who had almost no voice in recorded history: the poor of nineteenth-century Albany.

Excavation began in February 2002. Workers erected large tents over part of the site to provide heat for the team of up to 140 people, including professional archaeologists and anthropologists and many college-student volunteers.

To uncover the cemetery, workers used a backhoe to remove several inches of earth at a time until the dark shape of a burial shaft was observed. After a worker flagged the burial, an archaeologist began removing dirt by hand, scraping it away until the outline of the coffin was visible. Then the coffin was assigned a burial number and drawn onto a large site map showing its location. An archaeologist photographed the coffin lid before removing it and carefully uncovering the skeleton. Next, at least one sketch and a photograph were made of each burial and any artifacts found with it. Finally, an anthropologist would quickly examine the skeleton, noting anything unusual or striking about it, before the bones were removed and studied more carefully in the site's temporary laboratory.

In the lab, anthropologists tried to determine the age, sex, height, and ancestry of each person, though this was not always possible. Most of the recovered skeletons were in poor condition, because the cemetery was positioned above a layer of dense clay; the earth around the graves had no drainage, which caused the cemetery—and the coffins—to be saturated with water. The wet bones softened and crumbled, many dissolving into soggy pieces. Each skeleton was allowed to dry for two days so it would harden enough to be cleaned and studied further.

Within a month, the team had located almost three hundred bodies. Suddenly,

All of the burials excavated from the cemetery were numbered. This photograph shows Burial 802, a fifty-to-sixty-year-old woman who died around 1915.

Burial 318 was approximately sixty-five years old when he died. His body was used for teaching purposes at the nearby Albany Medical College before it was buried in the almshouse cemetery.

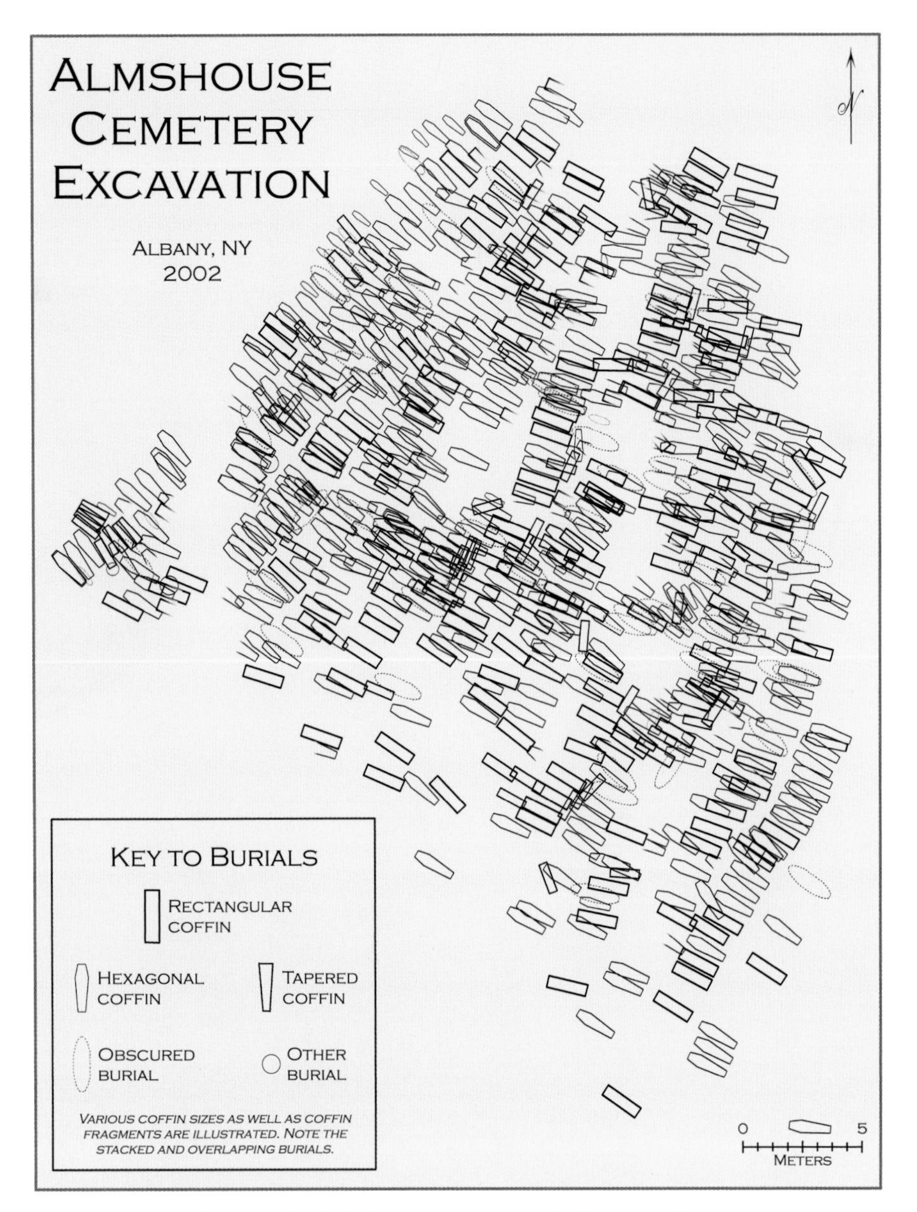

This map shows the many burials that were uncovered; the rows of graves appear somewhat haphazard and often contain many layers of burials.

everyone involved in the project realized that the building site had many more burials than anticipated. Some of the graves contained as many as five coffins stacked one atop the other, and twenty-two coffins held more than one body. By the time the project ended eight months later, 1,271 burials had been found—over five times the original estimate.

Anthropologists recorded anything abnormal that they saw on each skeleton. Using information from the skeletons and from the 1880–1926 burial records, they were able to determine the main causes of death for people who had lived in the almshouse and for those who had lived elsewhere, most likely in the city of Albany. Almshouse residents most often died from respiratory diseases, such as tuberculosis and pneumonia, or from what doctors then called "old age." People who had lived outside the almshouse frequently died more tragic deaths, such as from drowning, accidents, or suicide.

The burials revealed many details about the lives and deaths of the poor in nineteenth-century Albany. But the archaeologist Andrea Lain from the New York State Museum also wanted to give a more complete picture of the people from the almshouse cemetery.

For this reason, she asked the sculptor Gay Malin, who had reconstructed the face of Pearl from colonial Albany, to reconstruct some of their faces. Because the poor drainage had damaged most of the skeletons, only nine skulls were preserved well enough to allow reconstruction. Malin sculpted their faces so that museum-goers would be able to visualize these otherwise anonymous people.

One of the nine, a fifty-to-sixty-year-old woman, identified as Burial 802, revealed noticeable signs of violence. Her reconstructed face shows a severe injury to her forehead (either from an accident or a fight) that occurred long enough before her death around 1915 that it had healed. Her nose, broken more than once, was bent. For much of her life, though, she had worked hard. Her arm bones had strong muscle attachments and her spine and lower legs had arthritis; these conditions suggested to scientists that she may have worked as a scrubwoman. Her bones, however, did not reveal a cause of death.

A man known as Burial 318 showed researchers that some bodies were used for

Burials at the Almshouse Cemetery

Although burial records from 1880–1926 were hard to read and often incomplete, they provide a glimpse of the tragedies that the poor suffered at the time:

1888	Mary Lammidge	drowned in Nor. Kill Creek
1890	Baby Simmons	stillborn
1892	Skeleton of a child	found at 76 Grand St.
1899	Jennie	found in Erie Canal
1907	Patrick Roach	dead at Wm. Iyo's Saloon 73 Dove St.
1908	H. Dubois	found dead—Schlitz Hotel
1909	Rosario Del Fapola	shot himself and girl on Herkimer St.
1909	Bernard Cain	Crushed thigh and foot on NYCRR
1913	Juan Arias	drowned in River at Coeymans, NY
1924	Joseph Kelley	suicide Penitentiary

The "Lunatic Asylum" at the Albany County Almshouse

In 1949, the Time-Life photographer Jerry Cooke photographed residents of an infirmary (or poorhouse) in Indiana where older people with mental illness were housed because there was nowhere else to place them. Conditions at the Albany County Almshouse "lunatic asylum" visited by Dorothea Dix in 1842 would have been much worse.

In November 1842, Dorothea Dix, a crusader for mental health reform, made an unannounced visit to the Albany County Almshouse, where she told the administrator that she wanted to see the residents of the "lunatic asylum."

"No, you can't," he told her. "They're naked, in the crazy-cellar . . . you can't see them."

She persisted and was eventually taken to women's quarters of the asylum. In their shared room, she saw "several females chiefly in a state of dementia . . . decently dressed, but otherwise exhibited personal neglect . . . the hot air, foul with noisome vapors, produced a sense of suffocation and sickness impossible to be long endured."

Next she asked to be taken to the "crazy-cellars," where the most disturbed patients were locked away. After an argument, the man in charge of the dungeons let her inside. She made her way to a narrow hallway lined on each side by small rooms or cells; they were "totally dark and unventilated, and there was then no provision for drying or warming them."

> ***In the cell first opened was a madman: . . . a hideous object; matted locks, unshorn beard, a wild wan countenance, yet more disfigured by vilest uncleanness, in a state of entire nudity, save the irritating incrustations derived from that dungeon. . . . Here without light, without pure air, without warmth, without cleansing, without anything to secure decency or comfort, here was a human being, forlorn, abject, and disgusting it is true, but not the less a human being.***

Through Dix's efforts to correct the "brutalizing conditions of the most helpless of human beings," the asylum at Albany County Almshouse was somewhat improved. When she revisited it a year later, she found "the crazy-cellar" still crowded, but now the accommodations had nicer beds. She noted, though, that some male patients continued to be "chained to the beds or the floor."

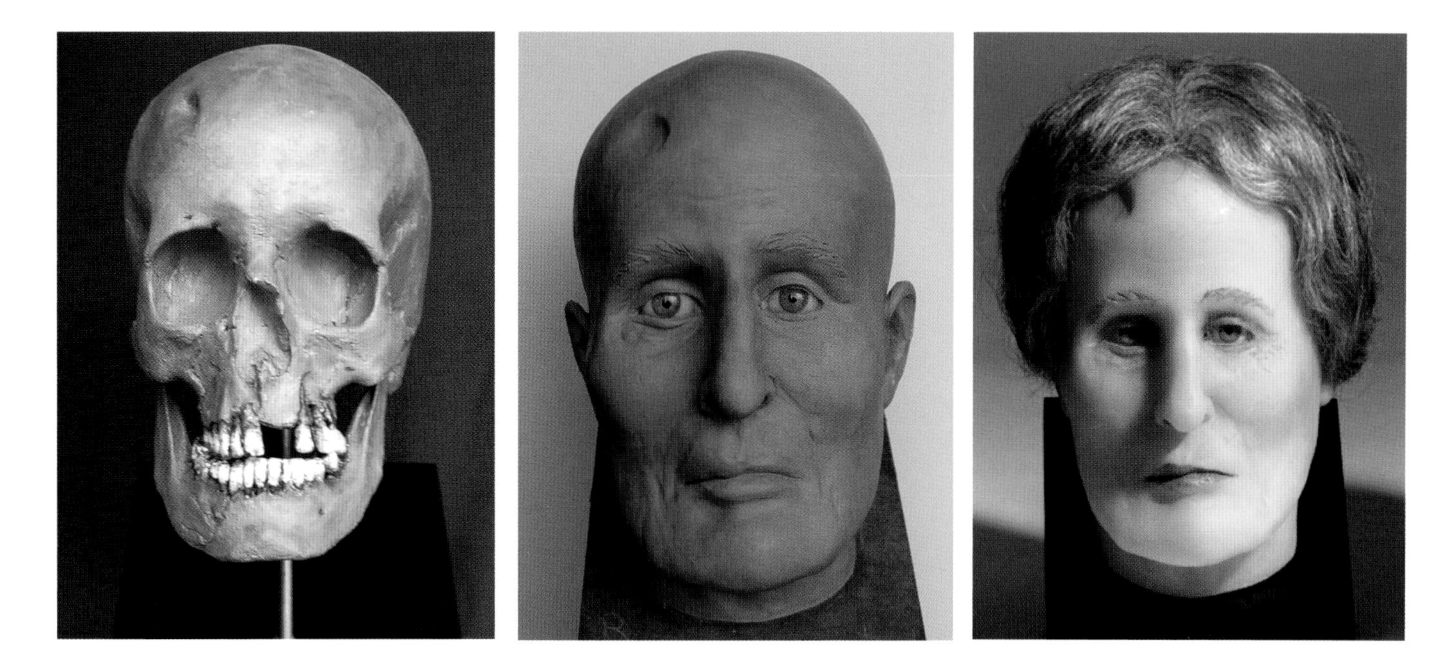

Although an analysis of Burial 802 did not indicate a cause of death, the woman's skeleton showed signs of repeated violence and hard work.

another purpose after death. The oldest of the nine people whose faces were reconstructed, he was about sixty-five when he died around 1900. His skeleton revealed that he had severe and long-term infections in his legs, sinuses, and skull. Because his bones indicated that he was quite muscular, anthropologists wondered if he could have been a dockworker, a common occupation in Albany at the time.

But they also noticed something more disturbing: His skull had been crudely autopsied. The top portion had been cut open at one point after his death. Researchers weren't surprised, since the Albany Medical College was located near the almshouse. Although medical schools today use donated cadavers to help teach their students about human anatomy, this was not the case when the almshouse was in use. In fact, beginning in 1854, New York State permitted unclaimed corpses to be used as specimens in anatomy labs. In 1894, the state also granted the Albany Medical College permission to collect corpses from the almshouse. Burial records from 1894 to 1926 indicated that the college had taken 312 bodies from the almshouse, 308 unclaimed bodies from the City of Albany, and 74 bodies from the penitentiary for teaching purposes.

Burial 318 may well have been one of them. The anthropologist Martin Solano, who studied the remains from the almshouse, found that most of the bodies taken by the medical college were not returned for burial. Only six bodies were given burial numbers, although archaeologists found fifty-one skeletons with autopsy marks on

The Reconstruction of the Almshouse People

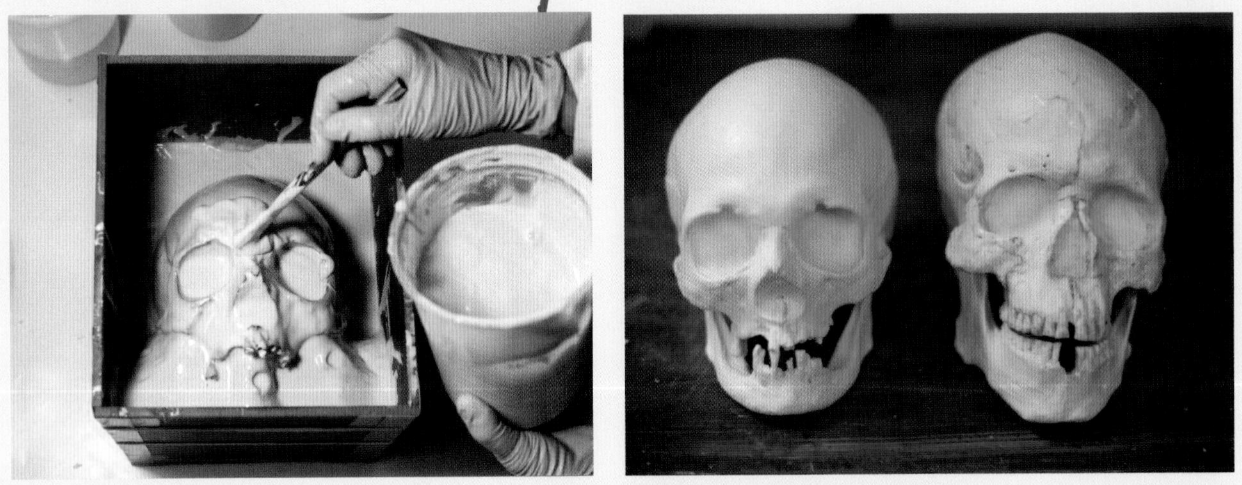

Gay Malin first made a mold of each skull (left), which allowed her to make resin copies of the skulls (right).

After Gay Malin determined the thickness of each person's facial tissue by using appropriate tables of tissue depths for age, gender, and ancestry, she placed tissue-depth pegs onto one copy of each skull. For guidance as she worked, she referred to the extra copy (left). She added facial muscles to the skull (right), then sculpted the final face. Next, she made another mold and cast the finished face out of a waxy resin, which made it look quite natural. Relying on suggestions from historians about hairstyles and garments of the period, Malin added appropriate hair and clothing.

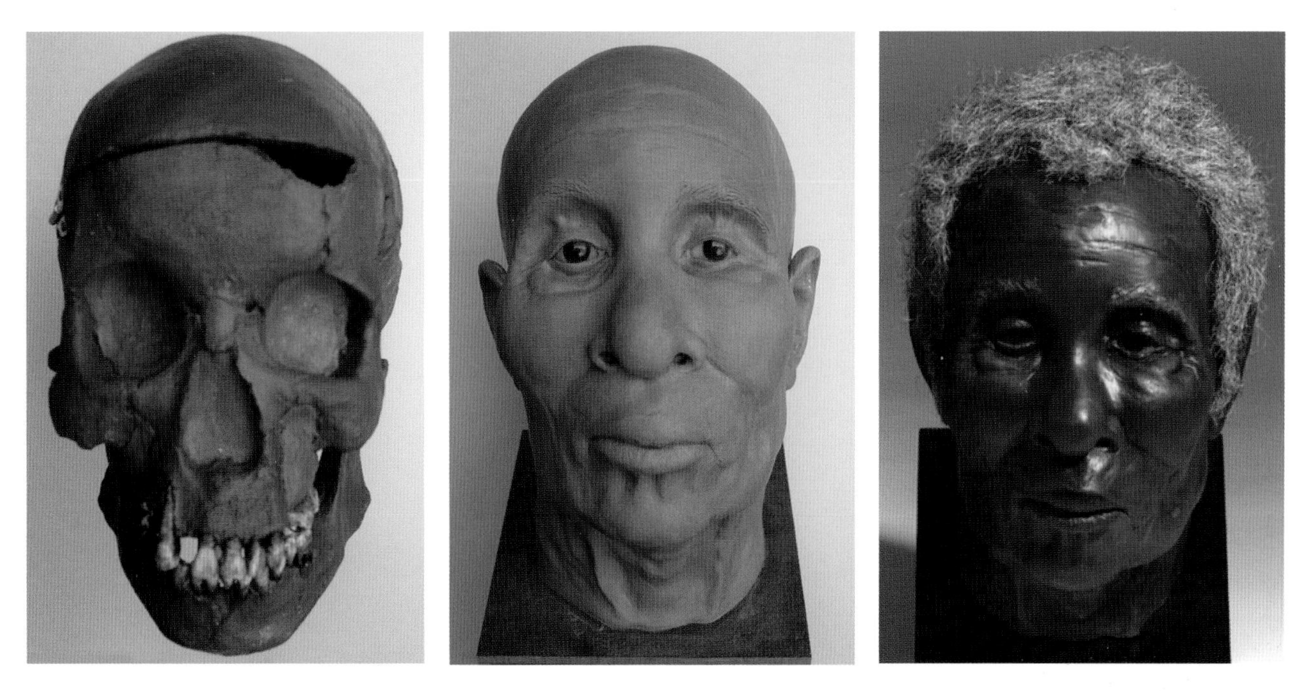

them. Burial 318, whose name and identity were not recorded anywhere, was one of the few who was given a proper, if late, burial. The top of his skull was also replaced before he was buried.

Burial 318 was not buried until after his body had been used by students at the Albany Medical College. His skull had been cut open during an anatomy lesson.

Even the coffins of the Albany County Almshouse cemetery provided information.

Two main types of coffin were used for burial: hexagonal and rectangular. Hexagonal coffins, archaeologists concluded, had been used to bury almshouse residents. They had been constructed especially for the deceased person, since there was almost no extra space inside them, regardless of how large or small the person was. Researchers found bills for coffin nails and lumber in almshouse records, as well as an old insurance map that showed the position of a carpenter's shed with an attached morgue on the premises; both discoveries indicated that an almshouse carpenter had built coffins. Hexagonal coffins also contained very few artifacts, except white buttons that had been used to fasten underwear. This suggested that the hexagonal burials were almshouse residents, who had almost no possessions and who were buried wearing only their undergarments. Finally, the hexagonal coffins were also buried deeper in the cemetery and therefore dated from an earlier time. In trying to locate information that would explain why fewer almshouse residents were buried in the cemetery over time, researchers found documents indicating that more relatives began to claim their bodies for burial elsewhere.

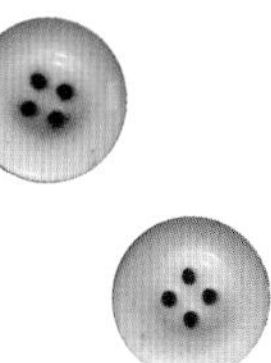

The only items found in the coffins of people who were living in the Albany County Almshouse when they died were small white buttons that had been used to fasten their underclothes. Anyone living in the almshouse would have had few, if any, possessions.

When the iron coffin with its viewing window (above) was found and opened, an archaeologist sketched the remains found inside as part of the recovery process (below).

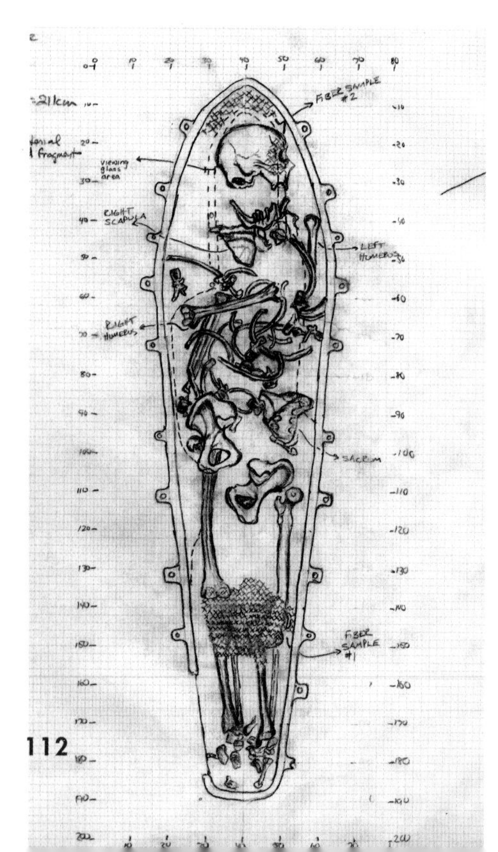

Rectangular coffins, however, told a different story about people who may have died outside the almshouse, often under tragic circumstances—unknown and unclaimed. Closer to the surface, the rectangular coffins were buried later in the cemetery's lifetime, as Albany delivered more unidentified bodies to the almshouse cemetery. The coffins themselves were cheaply made, a sign that there was a limited amount in the city budget for such burials. Some bodies were even interred in the wooden packing crates that had contained rectangular coffins, a further cost savings. A final sign that these burials came from outside the almshouse were the contents of the coffins; the people buried in rectangular coffins wore street clothes and had more possessions, such as coins and jewelry, with them. Clearly, they had not been almshouse residents.

Perhaps the most interesting discovery concerned the coffin of a woman (Burial IM) nicknamed "the Iron Maiden" by archaeologists for her iron coffin. About forty years old at the time of her death, she probably died from an infection caused by a badly abscessed tooth, anthropologists believe.

Her cast-iron coffin proved to be a huge mystery; it was quite unusual and dated from a much earlier time than the woman's death. Iron coffins were, in fact, popular during the Civil War but had fallen out of favor by the time the woman died.

Andrea Lain considered two possibilities to account for the coffin. Could the woman, she wondered, have died of such a terrible contagious disease that she was placed in a special coffin? Or did the funeral director simply want to dispose of an unfashionable type of coffin that he could no longer sell?

In the end, Lain could not solve the mystery, but Burial IM had left a lasting impression on everyone who saw her casket.

When the last body had been studied, the people from the almshouse cemetery were buried one final time in Section 48 of

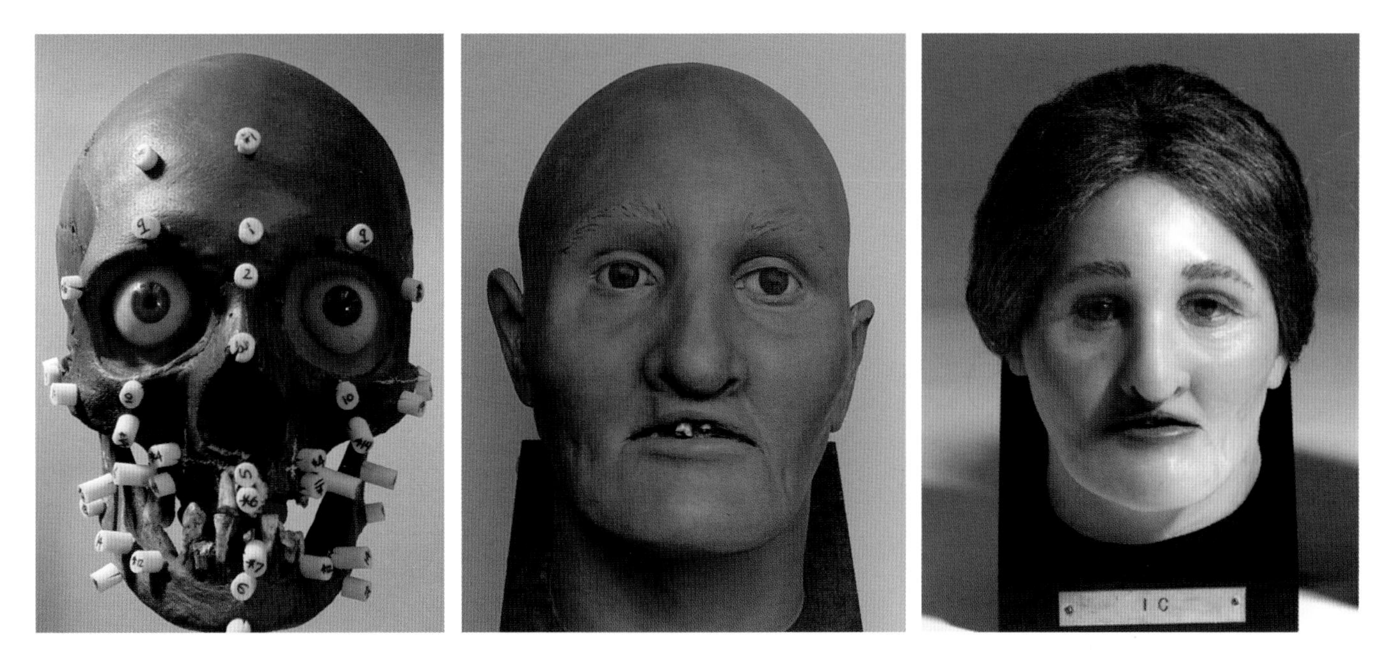

The sculptor Gay Malin reconstructed the face of the woman known as "the Iron Maiden." Her death was likely caused by a terribly abscessed tooth.

the Albany Rural Cemetery. Their tombstone reads HERE LIE THOSE ONCE BURIED IN THE ALBANY COUNTY ALMSHOUSE CEMETERY, TRANSFERRED TO THIS SITE 2002 A.D. A stanza from the Walt Whitman poem "Whispers of Heavenly Death" appears at the bottom:

Let me glide noiselessly forth;
With the key of softness unlock the locks—with a whisper,
Set ope the doors, O Soul!

The remains from the excavated graves at the almshouse cemetery were reburied together at the Albany Rural Cemetery.

Born in the Almshouse

In January 1869, Frank Baldwin was born in the Albany County Almshouse. His mother, a factory worker, was unable to care for him. Shortly before his first birthday, he was transferred from the almshouse to the Albany Orphanage Asylum, where he lived until he was ten. At that time, he was given his first indentured job. At thirteen he received a second job, this one on the farm of Philip Jones. Two years later Mr. Jones wrote to the director of the orphanage complaining about Frank's attitude:

I have tried my best and cant make him mind for when I need him moast he is mad and wont work. I cannot trust him to do chores to the barn without I am there to see to it. . . . one morning Frank . . . wouldent eat breakfast. my wife called him four or five times to come and eat. he would say I wont do it. she picked up a whip and whiped him. I told him to cary some milk away, he said I wont do it. I said go get some water and help me . . . , he said I wont do it. he sat in the barn and on the lot and dident have breakfast, Dinner, or supper. . . . we have whiped him three times. whiping does no good or nothing else. . . . I think you can manage Frank better in the sylum than any where else. . . . Please answer very soon.

The director reminded Mr. Jones that he was required to care for Frank until he could find another person to take him. When he was sixteen, Frank was placed with a farmer named Mr. Burley. After two years, Frank ran away and returned to Mr. Jones's farm. Frank himself wrote to the director of the orphanage to explain what happened:

These boys were residents of the Albany Orphanage Asylum around 1900.

I have left Frank Burley. . . . I could not stay with him for he did not give me clothes suitable for this cold weather, nothing but thin pants and old shoes, all to pieces. my feet were wet and cold. I took a severe cold and have it yet. . . . When I came to Mr. Jones, Mrs. Jones mended some clothes they had for me to put on & Mr. Jones got me a pair of boots. Mr. Fuller will you please see Burley & have him pay me for my work.

Yours Truly,
Frank Baldwin

That was the last correspondence between Frank and the orphanage. What happened to him? Did he live a long and happy life? No other details are known.

Although Fort Craig was the largest southwestern fort in 1861, it fell into ruin after it was deactivated in 1885. Because most of its buildings were constructed from adobe, little of the fort remains. This building, made of local stone, housed the commanding officer.

CHAPTER 9

THOMAS SMITH, *Buffalo Soldier*

He was young, finally free from slavery, and living in a desolate place far from home. Then he contracted cholera and died. He was buried in an army cemetery, but when it was relocated, he and many others were left behind and forgotten. Then one day the grave robbers found him and decided to steal his body.

An ordinary day in November 2004 suddenly turned unforgettable for the archaeologists Jeff Hanson and Mark Hungerford. That's when a historian named Don Alberts walked into their government office in Albuquerque, New Mexico, and began to tell them a story about a man he called "Gravedigger."

According to Alberts, one night during the early 1970s, Gravedigger and some friends camped out at a long-abandoned army fort in rural New Mexico. Built in 1853, Fort Craig was the largest southwestern fort by 1861. Eventually covering 149 acres and housing up to two thousand men and civilians, it saw fighting during the Civil War; shortly afterward its troops provided security for stagecoaches and nearby settlers. In 1885, when that protection was no longer needed, the fort was permanently deactivated. On two different occasions the army relocated burials from the cemetery, in 1876 to Santa Fe, New Mexico, and in 1886 to Leavenworth, Kansas. Once it was abandoned, the fort, built mostly from adobe, disintegrated in the wind and rain and became a neglected ruin.

An expert researcher, Gravedigger was aware that the army had removed the bodies from the coffins and relocated them long ago. He wondered aloud to his friends if any artifacts, such as buttons or coins, remained in the emptied coffins. Intrigued, the men began to search the old cemetery, about the size of a football field, for artifacts. Although the cemetery was on federal land and disturbing it was against the law, the men returned week after week and continued their looting.

On one occasion, when Gravedigger and his friends opened a coffin, they found a body along with the artifacts. The man had been buried in his uniform; by the looks of his hair and skin, they realized that he was African American. In fact, Fort Craig had been one of the first army forts to post

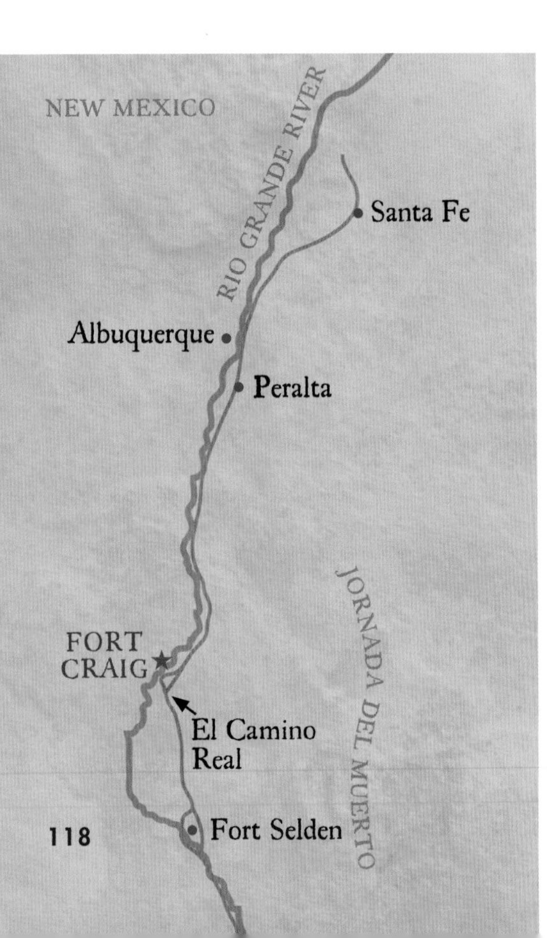

Fort Craig was at the northern end of a trail called *Jornada del muerto,* or Journey of Death. Because this stretch of the Camino Real, the old route of the Spanish conquistadors, was a shortcut that bypassed the bend of the Rio Grande, it also meant that travelers would not have access to water for the ninety-mile journey to Fort Selden, the next army fort.

This 1890 photograph shows buffalo soldiers of the Twenty-Fifth Infantry Regiment stationed in Fort Keogh, Montana. After the Civil War, African Americans made up one-fifth of the United States Army.

buffalo soldiers—African American soldiers who served in one of the all-black regiments of the United States Army after the Civil War. Their original mission was to maintain the peace on the western frontier, particularly in the wars against Indian tribes. They were soon given the nickname "buffalo soldiers" by the Comanche or the Cheyenne Indians, who respected their courage and determination and thought that their hair resembled the coat of a buffalo.

Although Gravedigger was an army veteran himself and had served in Vietnam, he thought nothing of removing the soldier's body from the coffin and taking it home as a kind of macabre trophy. He was even able to identify the man from an old army burial map of the cemetery. The soldier was Private Thomas Smith, from the 125th United States Colored Infantry, which had been stationed at Fort Craig during 1865–67.

Knowing the man's identity didn't stop Gravedigger from displaying Private Smith's head on his fireplace mantel along with an assortment of other human remains that he had looted: two more skulls, an amputated limb, and the shackled legs of a skeleton. The headless soldier's body was kept in a fifty-five-gallon barrel elsewhere on his property.

Ten years after the body was stolen from the cemetery, the historian Don Alberts, who had become a friend of Gravedigger's, saw the remains for the first time. By then, most of Gravedigger's family and friends—including some local archaeologists and college professors—also knew that the mummified remains had been stolen and openly displayed in his house, but no one reported his crime until some thirty years later, when Alberts finally told the archaeologists in 2004.

In 2007 archaeologists excavated the cemetery of Fort Craig in order to stop any further looting. Each rectangle below is the location of a coffin.

The archaeologists Hanson and Hungerford were so disturbed by the story that they wanted to see Gravedigger brought to justice for his crime. But Gravedigger was dying. Although Alberts had urged him to return the stolen corpse of Private Smith while he was still alive, he had made no attempt to do so. By the time Hanson and Hungerford were able to visit the cemetery at Fort Craig, they learned that Gravedigger—whose name was Dee Brecheisen—had died without returning the body.

In February 2005 federal authorities began an investigation in hopes of recovering Smith's body. They interviewed Brecheisen's friends and family, looking for substantive clues. Finally, in the late afternoon of April 25, 2005, an archaeological-crime investigator named Noel Wagner learned from an informant that the body of Thomas Smith would be placed outside Dee Brecheisen's family home in Peralta, New Mexico. Wagner called Hanson and Hungerford and asked them to meet him at the house and identify the remains.

A short time later, Wagner drove up to the house expecting to find a barrel with Smith's body inside, but all he saw was a brown paper grocery bag sitting beneath a tree. He picked it up and carried it to his truck. Then he waited until a medical examiner, Hanson, and Hungerford arrived. When the bag was finally opened, they found an object nestled inside two brightly printed paper towels: the head of an African American man that was so well preserved that the hair and skin were still attached to the skull.

The next day federal investigators, armed with a warrant, searched Brecheisen's house, hoping to find Smith's body and evidence of looting at Fort Craig. Inside, they discovered many items looted from Native American burial sites and other abandoned army forts, but little that had come from Fort Craig and no sign of Private Smith's body. Investigators learned that most of Brecheisen's illegal collection had been sold to other collectors shortly after he died. They wondered if Smith's body had been sold or given to a collector. Although the deceased Brecheisen could not be charged with a crime, anyone who had possession of Private Smith's body could be.

As investigators pursued and then closed the investigation for lack of evidence, archaeologists decided to excavate the Fort Craig cemetery. They believed that they would find other burials that had not been relocated. By removing any forgotten remains and artifacts, they would make certain that not only would the person receive a proper burial in another army cemetery but the graves would never be looted again. Of course, they also hoped that they might find the missing body of Thomas Smith.

With no publicity, archaeologists conducted two excavations at Fort Craig: the first in 2005, followed by another in 2007. Altogether, the excavations uncovered 221 mostly empty coffins, but the army had somehow failed in 1885 to relocate sixty-four intact burials: twenty-six infants and children and thirty-eight adults, including four women. Archaeologists also found two surgeon's pits, which contained amputated limbs, most likely from surgeries performed after the Civil War battle of Val Verde, which was fought near the fort.

A carefully crafted small coffin contained the remains of an infant holding a small bouquet of flowers.

Mark Hungerford, who excavated twenty-two of the burials himself, recalled removing a small, well-made coffin that contained the tiny skeleton of an infant. It was taken back to a lab in Albuquerque, where it was opened. Inside was a well-preserved baby, wearing a tiny gown, its hands crossed upon its chest, holding a small bunch of flowers.

In May 2009 the thirty-eight adult burials were shipped in a rental van to the Smithsonian Institution in Washington, D.C., for a two-month study before they were

This coffin contains an intact burial of a teenage boy. There were no artifacts or clothing, and an analysis of the skeleton did not reveal the cause of death.

scheduled for reburial. Their bones were measured, x-rayed, and CT-scanned as Smithsonian scientists tried to establish age, height, ancestry, and any diseases or trauma that were evident. The analysis showed that the thirty-eight adults had died of many causes: "murders, suicides, fatal accidents, and disease: typhoid, cholera, dysentery, and smallpox." Eleven of the adults had African American ancestry.

Four of the burials taken to the Smithsonian were missing their skulls, a probable sign of looting. One day later, a graduate-student researcher at the Smithsonian named Alaina Goff was examining Thomas Smith's skull when she had a brainstorm. She took Smith's head and held it up to each of the four headless skeletons that were laid out on examining tables. The skeletons of the first three were much too large to accommodate Smith's smaller skull. But when she placed it onto the fourth skeleton, she found that it fit perfectly.

At last, Thomas Smith was whole again. His disarticulated skeleton had been dumped back into his coffin at some point. Now his complete skeleton could receive a proper burial.

By this time, researchers had located more information about Private Smith. Many early buffalo soldiers had been slaves before they joined the army, and Thomas Smith was no exception. Enslaved to a Kentucky farmer named William Smith, Thomas Smith enlisted in early 1865 in the 125th U.S. Colored Infantry, Company A, without his owner's consent. Like other enlistees, he had to agree to serve for three years. During his first eighteen months of service in Kentucky, he was assigned

This coffin was looted by grave robbers. The skeleton was removed and replaced later, without the skull. This proved to be the body of Private Thomas Smith.

duties as an orderly, delivering messages and running errands for officers. In August 1866, however, his regiment began its journey to New Mexico, where the troops were assigned to a series of forts along the Rio Grande.

A frail young man standing only five feet, two inches tall, Smith arrived at Fort Craig in late September 1866. The fort was a dusty, dirty, and unsanitary place. Although privies were built around it, they filled up quickly and were not always cleaned out or rebuilt in a timely fashion. In June 1864, with no privies available, the commanding officer had written that the troops in the fort "committed 'nuisances' in all directions outside the south wall 'presenting a most revolting sight.' " More

This photograph of Fort Craig, taken around 1866 by the United States Army Signal Corps, shows the adobe soldiers' quarters in the background and the dusty landscape inside the fort itself.

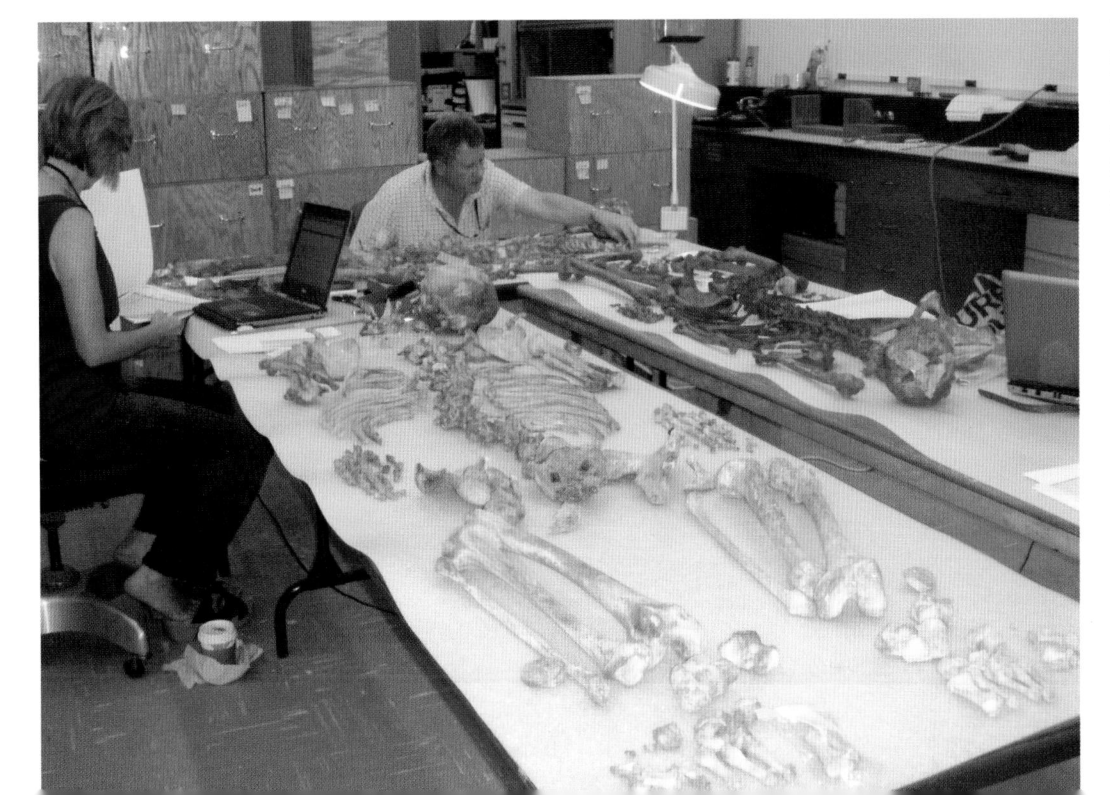

The remains of four skeletons were examined at the Smithsonian Institution in May 2009.

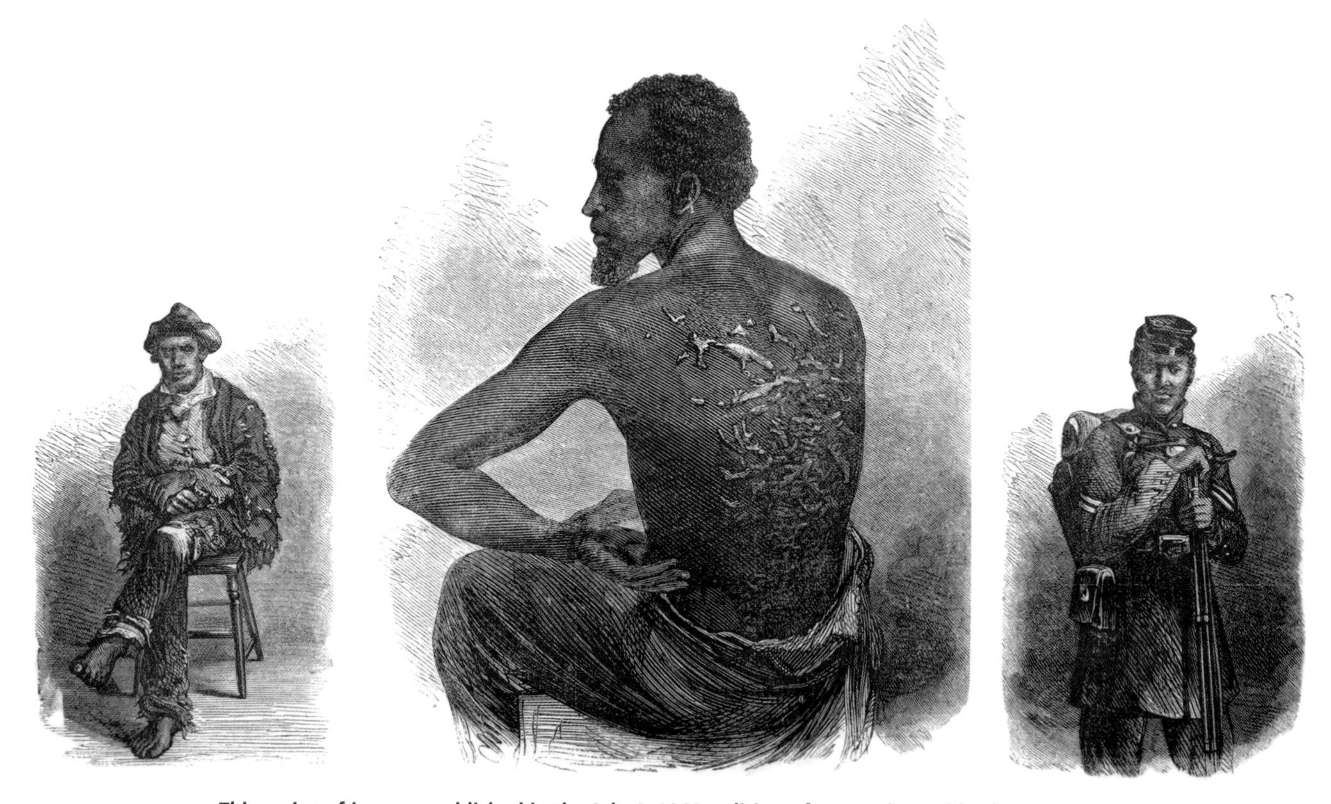

This series of images, published in the July 4, 1863, edition of *Harper's Weekly,* shows a man named Gordon who escaped from slavery in Louisiana to join the United States Army. The artist illustrated his appearance when he arrived at the recruitment center, his scarred back revealed during his physical examination, and his new look in an army uniform.

privies were built, but inadequate sanitation continued to plague the fort. The stables and corral, located within the fort's walls, contributed to the filth. Animal waste was "often distinctly perceptible on the parade ground, and mosquitoes and flies [were] attracted in great numbers, to the discomfort of the garrison." Finally, the cloudy water from the Rio Grande was the only source for drinking and cooking; during warm weather, the troops also bathed in it.

Smith became ill at the fort soon after he arrived and was admitted to the hospital twice, first in late September and then at the end of October. He died at 2:45 a.m. on November 21, 1866, of cholera, a common disease then. At that time doctors believed that cholera was caused by "impurities in the air." For that reason, army doctors were required to monitor "the weather on a daily basis . . . recording . . . high and low temperatures, precipitation, cloud cover, wind velocity, and wind direction." Doctors now know that cholera is often caused by drinking water or eating food that is contaminated with the cholera bacterium. Clearly, there were many opportunities for water and food to become contaminated at Fort Craig.

Both his death and the looting of his body more than a hundred years later were tragedies. But the excavation of the cemetery revealed that Private Thomas Smith was no longer alone. Of the sixty-four remains recovered by archaeologists, investigators were eventually able to identify the bodies of two other buffalo soldiers buried at Fort Craig: Levi Morris and David Ford.

In late June 2009, sixty-one human remains were buried at the National Cemetery in Santa Fe, New Mexico. A month later, on July 28, the remaining three—the buffalo soldiers Thomas Smith, Levi Morris, and David Ford—were reburied there as well, with full military honors. All were placed in handmade coffins.

The memorial marker erected by the graves tells that the sixty-four individuals were recovered from the Fort Craig cemetery. "Of these," the marker continues, "the identities of three persons were documented, the others remain unknown. May they never again be forgotten. Rest in peace. July 2009."

The memory of the three soldiers would be honored in another, unique way.

On July 28, 2009, members of the Tucson, Arizona, Buffalo Soldiers Association served as pallbearers for Thomas Smith, Levi Morris, and David Ford. They were buried in handmade coffins.

Workers prepare to bury the remains of the sixty-one unknown individuals. Each small wooden box contained the remains of one person and was placed in a larger coffin for burial.

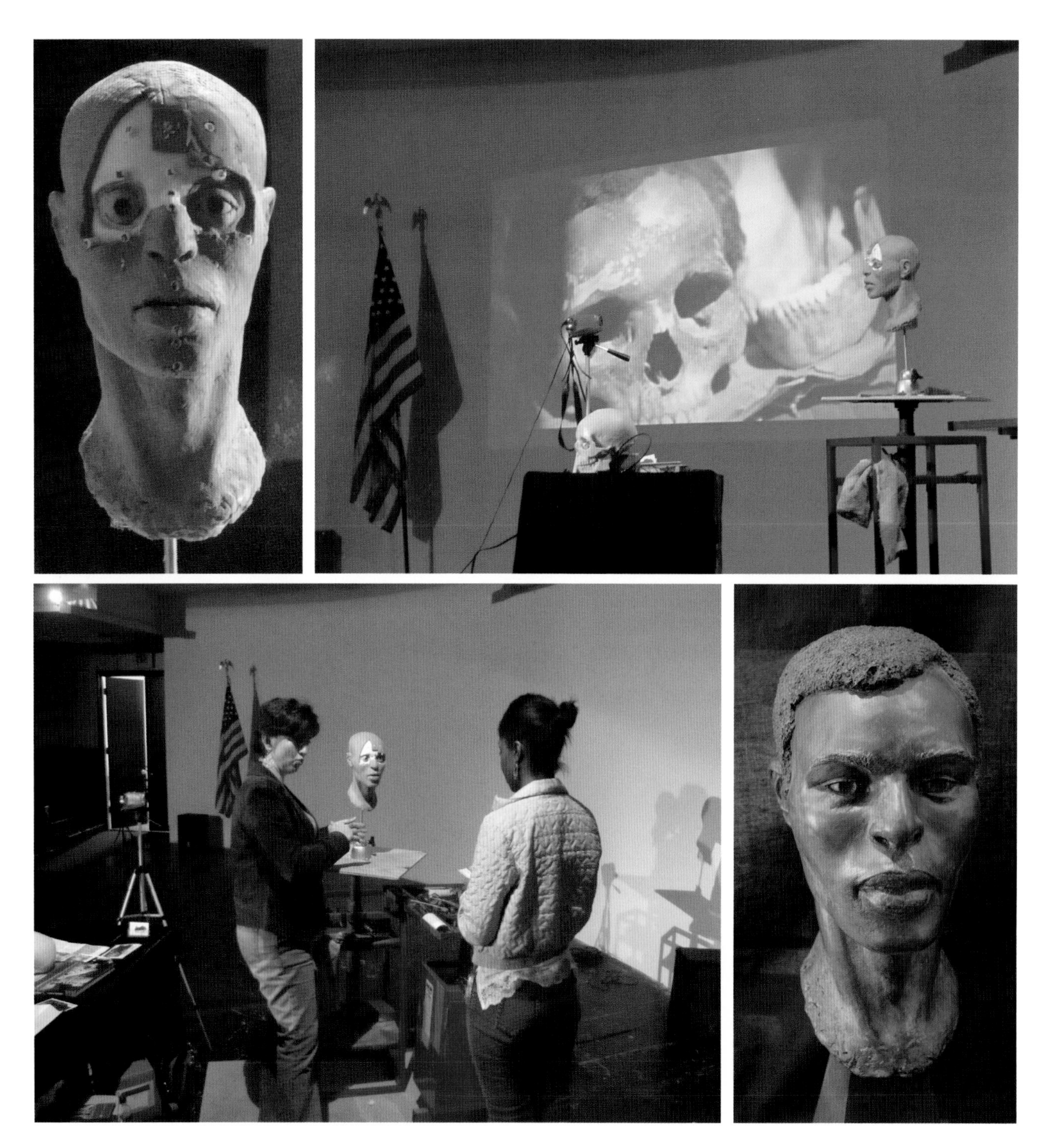

Amanda Danning reconstructed the face of Private Thomas Smith onstage during February 2010. As she worked, a film about the life, death, looting, and excavation of Thomas Smith was shown to the audience. Afterward audience members had a chance to question Danning about Smith and her work as an artist. She applied a bronze finish to the final cast so that it appeared to be made of metal.

The sculptor Amanda Danning, who had worked for the Smithsonian Institution, was asked by the Smithsonian and the Buffalo Soldiers National Museum in Houston to reconstruct the face of Thomas Smith to remind everyone of the forgotten buffalo soldiers of Fort Craig. Using the data from the CT scans done at the Smithsonian, replica skulls were created. Less than a year after the three men were reburied, in February 2010, Danning set up her sculpting equipment and warmed up her clay in an old theater near the Houston museum, where, for one month, she worked on the reconstruction as visitors watched.

When she was finished, the face of Thomas Smith went on exhibit at the Buffalo Soldiers National Museum—a reminder of everything he had experienced as a slave, a free man, a soldier, and a very sick young man.

Today Thomas Smith's grave (right) can be found at the National Cemetery in Santa Fe, New Mexico. Dee Brecheisen, who participated in the theft of Thomas Smith's remains and the looting of Fort Craig's cemetery, is buried in a quiet Kansas cemetery (below).

Buffalo Soldier Levi Morris

Levi Morris's skeleton remained undisturbed in the Fort Craig cemetery. *He had been buried with nickels placed on his eyelids; over time, they stained the area around his eyes green.*

Like Thomas Smith, Private Levi Morris was born into slavery in Vicksburg, Mississippi. After emancipation, he lived in Akron, Ohio, where he worked as a plasterer for a time. In December 1872 he enlisted in the Ninth Cavalry, Company B, in Pittsburgh, Pennsylvania. His company spent three years in south Texas, then eighteen months in New Mexico, to prevent Indian raids. He had only six months left to serve when his regiment was told it would be transferred from Fort Craig to Fort Bayard, also in New Mexico.

It was during the journey to Fort Bayard, while his company was camped near Round Mountain, New Mexico, that he and a soldier named Peter Johnson began to argue as they fried their day's ration of meat. According to Peter Johnson's statement recorded in his later court-martial, early in the morning of June 19, 1877, Private Morris "came up to the fire and took a piece of bacon out of [Johnson's] pan." Unaware that Morris had placed bacon in the same pan, Johnson thought Morris was stealing his meat and knocked it back into the pan.

Angered, Morris took a two-foot piece of dry firewood and struck Johnson on the back of the neck. Johnson was staggered by the blow and said, according to later testimony, "I did not know you had any meat in the pan."

Morris thought the incident was over and tried to retrieve his bacon. As he did, Johnson grabbed a nearby axe, swung it over his head, and in one swoop planted it in Private Morris's back. The axe broke three ribs and opened a deep, four-inch-long gash in Morris's back.

Taken back to the Fort Craig hospital, Morris was

given brandy and water every half hour, and his wound was regularly cleaned. He lingered for nine days. During this time he gave the assistant surgeon at the hospital a final statement. In part, it read: "I went to take my meat out of the mess pan and he [Peter Johnson] would not let me take it but snatched it from me. I hauled off and struck him with a club. He then walked round behind me and picked up the axe and struck me with it. I struck him across the back of the neck with the club, but not hard as I did not want to hurt him."

He signed the statement with his mark, since like many early buffalo soldiers he had not been legally allowed to learn how to read and write when he was a slave. He died on June 28, 1877, and was buried the same day in Grave 103. Peter Johnson was sentenced to life in a military prison, though his sentence was later reduced to seven years because, according to court-martial records, he had been struck first.

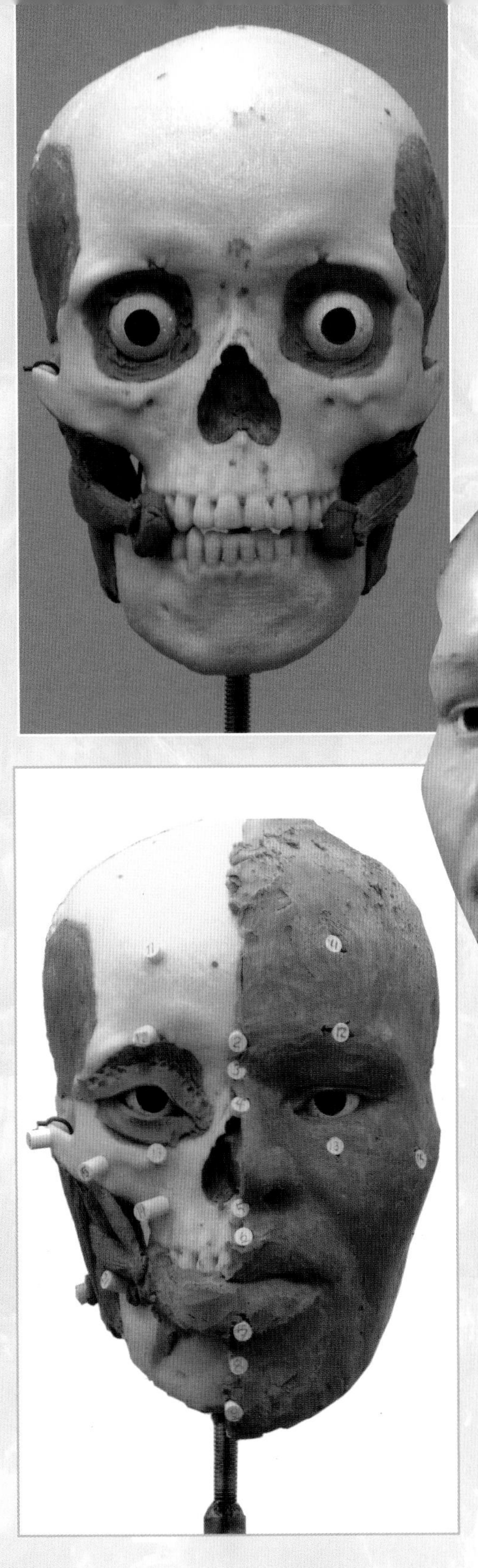

The face of Levi Morris (below) was reconstructed by Amanda Danning. She first applied muscle groups made of gray clay onto the skull (left top), then applied brown clay to the exact tissue depths required (left bottom).

The remains of the six Chinese miners are stored in acid-free cardboard boxes in the Human Remains Repository at the University of Wyoming's Department of Anthropology.

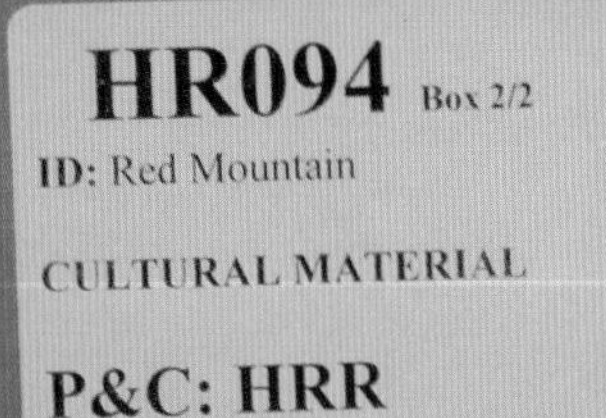

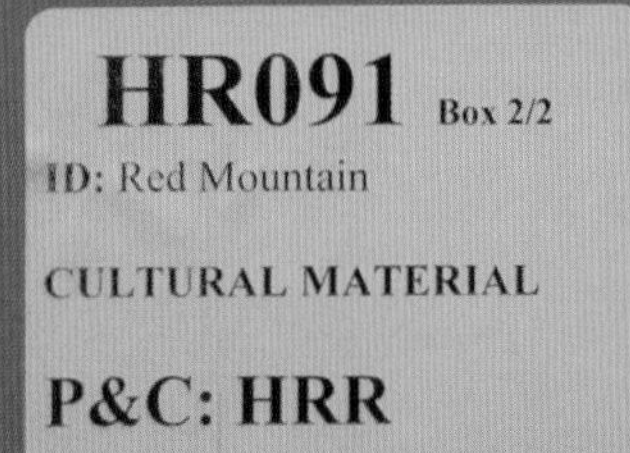

CHAPTER 10

SIX CHINESE MINERS *from Wyoming*

CIRCA

They came to North America to make their fortunes and died digging coal from the mines of Wyoming. But the lonely cemetery was lost over time. Some one hundred years later, construction workers uncovered them accidentally, reminding everyone of what the miners' hard work had accomplished.

Among the many boxes stored at the Human Remains Repository (HRR) of the University of Wyoming's Department of Anthropology, six are quite unusual. Labeled HR090 through HR095, they contain the skeletons of six individuals found in August 1982 by a construction crew laying a pipeline near Red Mountain on the outskirts of Evanston, Wyoming.

After being notified of the discovery, the Wyoming State Crime Laboratory removed the burials and sent them to its headquarters in Cheyenne. There they were examined by George W. Gill, a bioarchaeologist from the University of Wyoming. The style and hardware of the coffins, along with the individuals' clothing, indicated that the remains dated from the late 1800s. As a result, Professor Gill concluded that the six individuals were of historical but not criminal importance, and they were transferred to the HRR, where he systematically studied the remains.

He determined that the burials were men who ranged in age from about twenty-three to forty-eight and in height from almost five feet, two inches to five foot five. The men were in generally good health with no sign of physical injuries when they died. The only indication of poor health was in their teeth, a surprising result considering that 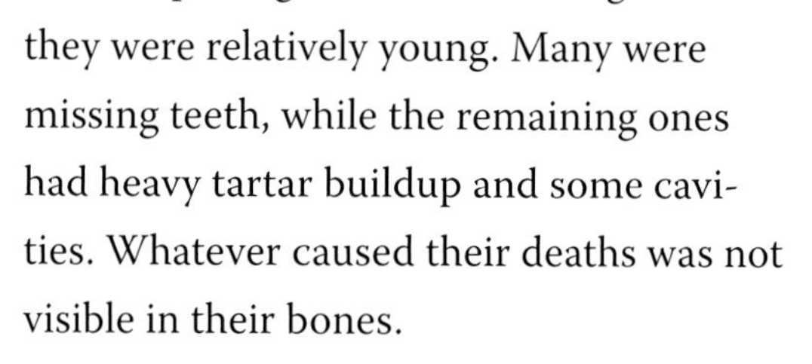 they were relatively young. Many were missing teeth, while the remaining ones had heavy tartar buildup and some cavities. Whatever caused their deaths was not visible in their bones.

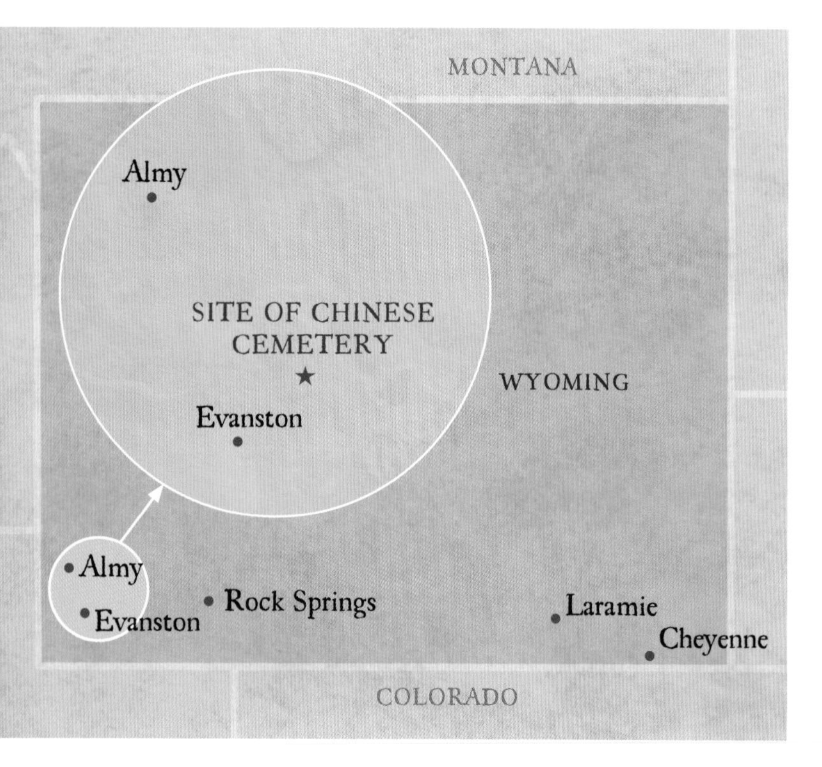

In late 1881, Chinese miners who died in the Almy mine explosion were buried in the Chinese cemetery north of Evanston.

Perhaps the most surprising discovery about the skeletons was their ancestry. When Gill examined their skulls, many features, including their prominent cheekbones, led him to conclude that they were of Chinese ancestry. But, he wondered, why would six Chinese men from the late 1800s be buried in an unmarked Wyoming cemetery?

Rennie Polidora, a graduate student, set out to answer that question by

When they died, Chinese immigrants in the western United States were buried in Chinese cemeteries, often found in remote and desolate areas.

researching the history of Chinese immigrants in the western United States. She learned that at the start of the California gold rush in 1848, many Chinese workers began to emigrate to the United States, hoping to make their fortune and return to China. By 1870, many Chinese workers had moved to other areas of the western frontier, helping to build the transcontinental railroad, then working in the mines that provided coal to run the locomotives. They worked under harsh conditions, often for lower pay than white workers, and usually lived together in crowded Chinatowns. Residents often looked down on them, and laws were enacted that discriminated against them. When they died, Chinese immigrants were usually not permitted to be buried in the local cemeteries; a separate Chinese burial ground was used, often on a remote and desolate piece of land.

Polidora also discovered that a small but substantial number of Chinese immigrants had worked as miners in western Wyoming during that time. A Chinese cemetery, long unmarked, had been located in the Evanston area, and that is what the construction crew had discovered.

With no apparent injuries on their skeletons, Polidora considered the possibility that the Chinese men had died of a disease, such as influenza or diphtheria, at about the same time. Many infectious diseases do not leave any telltale signs on a person's skeleton after death, so this was not unlikely. In examining local history books and newspapers about Evanston, Polidora learned that a diphtheria epidemic had swept through the

Chinese immigrants helped build the transcontinental railroad. During the summer of 1877, many Chinese laborers helped strengthen the curved trestle near Secret Town, California, by hauling dirt to fill in the river valley.

Local townspeople throughout the western United States looked upon Chinese immigrants with distrust. Here Chinese residents of Evanston, Wyoming, celebrate the Chinese new year in an undated photo.

The Chinese Exclusion Act (1882)

Before 1882 the United States had essentially had an open immigration policy. But as Chinese immigrants began to cross the Pacific seeking better economic opportunities, their willingness to work for lower wages angered "native-born Americans [who] attributed unemployment and declining wages to Chinese workers." As calls for an anti-immigration bill increased, a joint congressional committee held hearings at which many anti-Chinese witnesses spoke. Two health officials, for example, testified that "the Chinese were responsible for bringing leprosy and smallpox to California."

The passage of the Chinese Exclusion Act in 1882 prohibited Chinese from emigrating to the United States. It also prevented any Chinese people from becoming naturalized U.S. citizens. The act was extended for an additional ten years in 1892 and also "required all Chinese immigrants to register with the Internal Revenue Service and keep their identification papers with them all the time. Anyone who failed to do so would be deported." The act became permanent in 1904. On December 17, 1943, during World War II, the Chinese Exclusion Repeal Act was passed, although it permitted "only 105 Chinese immigrants per year" to enter the United States. Finally, in 1965, the Immigration Act allowed Chinese citizens—and many others from around the world—to emigrate to the United States in much larger numbers.

town and surrounding towns in 1885. But she was unable to reach a definite conclusion about their deaths.

Professor Rick Weathermon, who became the director of the Human Remains Repository a few years ago, also wondered about the six Chinese men. He knew that if they had died earlier than 1885, their deaths might have had another cause prevalent at the time: a mine explosion.

Most Chinese immigrants in the Evanston area worked in the coal mines of Almy, a small mining area a few miles north of Evanston. Many mining accidents had occurred over the years, and local newspapers reported a serious mine explosion in Almy on March 4, 1881:

> *A fearful explosion took place in mine No. 2 last night. The cause is not definitely known, but it is supposed to be by gas generated by fire in the abandoned mine No. 1, which has been burning for the past six years, and is separated from mine No. 2 by wide walls only. . . . There were sixty Chinamen and four white men in the mine. Of the latter, Mr. Gillespie, John Barton and Josiah Crosby were taken out dead, and Charles Beverage alive. . . . Twenty-five Chinamen have been brought to the surface, all badly scalded and many with broken limbs. The balance are probably dead. The*

Resentment of Chinese in Wyoming

Chinese workers came to Wyoming in small but increasing numbers from 1868 to 1885. Once they arrived, they ran headlong into racist attitudes. One Wyoming newspaper in Green River, the *Frontier Index,* proclaimed itself "an anti-Black, anti-Indian, and anti-Chinese newspaper" in 1868 and had as its motto "Only White Men to be naturalized in the United States." Even in 1870, however, only 143 Chinese immigrants resided in Wyoming. Ten years later, there were 914. After that, the number of Chinese residents began to decrease, and in 1930, Wyoming had only 130.

Although they were viewed as a threat to the local residents' livelihood, the Chinese were repeatedly hired as railroad workers and miners because they cost the owners less money and they were hard workers. After the transcontinental railroad was finished in 1869, an official of the Union Pacific "planned to discharge the 'Irishmen' and replace them with Chinese workers," which would reduce his labor costs by half.

White workers who were angry about losing their jobs often did not see the companies or their owners at fault. Instead, they blamed the Chinese workers.

This historical marker located near Almy recounts one of Wyoming's worst mining disasters, which took place on March 4, 1881. The six men found in Evanston may have died as a result of that explosion.

Although much of the coffin wood had decomposed, coffin handles and decorative plates indicated that three of the men had matching coffins.

> *white men were all married and leave large families. The fire in the mine is now out, and everything possible is being done for the recovery of the balance of bodies and for the injured.*

Another newspaper story reported, "About 20 dead Chinamen have been discovered, but have not yet been brought up."

Although at least thirty-eight Chinese miners died that night, their names were never published in newspaper reports. Many of them suffered burns or violent injuries in the explosion, but some probably died from asphyxiation when they were trapped in smoke-filled mine passages. Other newspaper accounts tell that the mining company provided coffins and burial garments for some of the Chinese dead. Weathermon wondered if this explained why three of the six burials recovered in Evanston had matching coffins and why five of the men wore similar western-style burial clothes, both signs that they might have died at the same time.

The burials of the six men have provided archaeologists and historians with a wealth of information about Chinese immigrants. For example, a metal lard bucket was found with HR093 and may have served as an inscription stone, sometimes called "an afterworld suitcase." Papers in or inscriptions on the bucket would have given the name of the person and information about his place of origin and relatives. Although almost all Chinese immigrants who worked on the railroad or in the mines expected to go back to China, they made instructions for their burial in case they died before they could return. Often they were to be buried for about seven years, so that the bodies would be completely decomposed. Then their skeletons would be dug up and cleaned by a paid bone collector for shipment back to China, where a final burial would take place. The information on or in the metal bucket would then be used by the bone collector to identify the body.

Despite the best efforts of Gill, Polidora, and Weathermon, the men remain unidentified. Today their skeletons are still stored at the University of Wyoming, where they will stay indefinitely. As with most historic skeletons that have been found, there are no plans to have a sculptor reconstruct their faces and show the world what the men looked like. But their remains—and the story behind them—are a reminder of the Chinese who emigrated to the West and whose hard work under difficult circumstances helped build the United States.

The skeletons were stored in boxes, while bulky items, such as clothing, were placed in acid-free bags for preservation (below). Five of the men wore western-style bow ties (below). The buttons from HR091 were marked "MODE DE PARIS" (bottom).

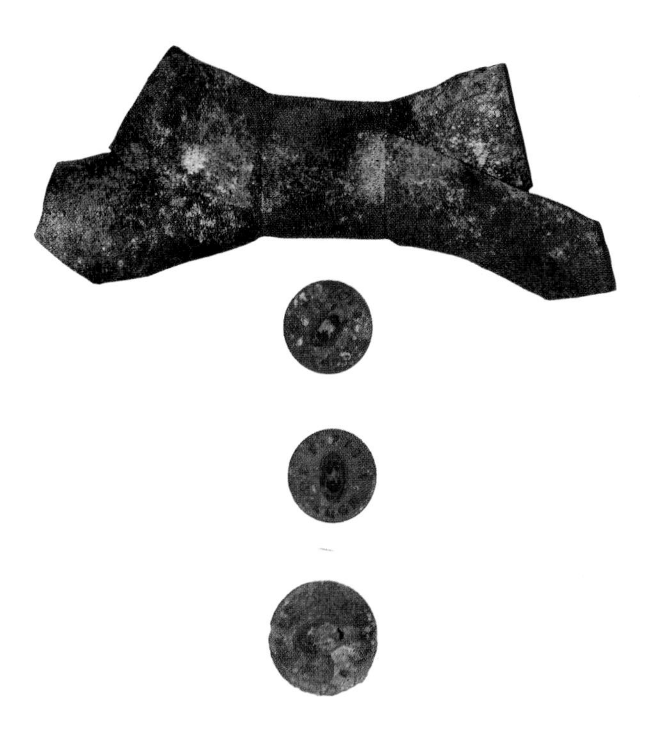

The Rock Springs Massacre

One of the most notorious episodes of anti-Chinese violence in the United States occurred in a coal-mining town named Rock Springs, Wyoming, not far from Evanston.

In the early morning of September 2, 1885, the resentment of some white miners in Rock Springs reached the boiling point. Accounts of the massacre differ, but what is known is that a small group of Chinese and white miners argued as work began in coal pit number 6. Then the white miners attacked and seriously injured three Chinese miners. Work was stopped, but the white miners began to assemble in a part of Rock Springs called "Whiteman's Town."

At two in the afternoon the white miners divided into three groups and headed for "Chinatown." According to one report of the incident, filed by the 559 Chinese laborers of Rock Springs:

> *Whenever the mob met a Chinese they stopped him and, pointing a weapon at him, asked him if he had any revolver, and then approaching him they searched his person, robbing him of his watch or any gold or silver . . . before letting him go. Some of the rioters would let a Chinese go after depriving him of all his gold or silver, while another Chinese would be beaten with the butt ends of the weapons before being let go. Some of the rioters, when they could not stop a Chinese, would shoot him dead on the spot.*

The mob told the Chinese that they had one hour to leave town. At around three, they attacked Chinatown, shooting unarmed Chinese residents and setting their houses afire. Some Chinese, afraid to leave, hid in their houses; others fled for their lives into the hills that outside the town. By the time the massacre ended, Chinatown was engulfed in flames, twenty-eight Chinese had been killed, and fifteen others had been wounded.

The Chinese counsel in New York, Huang Sih Chuen, traveled in mid-September to Rock Springs, where he thoroughly examined the bodies of the dead Chinese. His report, which gave a graphic accounting of the massacre, included a summary about each victim. Here are three:

> *The dead body of Leo Sun Tsung, found in his own hut in the native settlement, was covered with many wounds. The left jawbone was broken, evidently by a bullet. The skin and bone of the right leg below the knee were injured. I also ascertained that the deceased was fifty-one years old, and had a mother, wife, and son living at home (in China). . . .*
>
> *The dead body of Leo Dye Bah was found at the side of the bridge, near the creek, shot in the middle of the chest by a bullet, breaking the breastbone. I also ascertained that the deceased was fifty-six years old, and had a wife, son, and daughter at home.*
>
> *. . .*
>
> *A portion of the dead body of Sia Bun Ning was found in a pile of ashes in the hut near the Chinese temple. It consisted of the head, neck, and shoulders. The two hands, together with the rest of the body below the chest, were completely burned off. I also ascertained that the deceased was thirty-seven years old, and had a mother, wife, son, and daughter living at home.*

Although sixteen rioters were brought to trial, none were convicted. In fact, the foreman of the jury was a

In this engraving by the artist Thure de Thulstrup, Chinese miners flee for their lives from the 1885 massacre in Rock Springs, Wyoming. Based on photographs taken by Lieutenant C. A. Booth, the illustration was published in the September 24, 1886, issue of Harper's Weekly.

medical doctor who had also participated in the riot, "riding his horse, waving his hat, and shouting loudly . . . 'Shoot them down!'"

Although the Union Pacific, which owned the Rock Springs coal mines, continued to hire Chinese immigrants to work there and refused to rehire any white miners known to have participated in the massacre, eventually the small Chinese population of Wyoming began to move elsewhere.

But not all left.

One Chinese immigrant who remained was Pung Chung. In one of the few individual accounts of the massacre, published sixty-two years later, David G. Thomas, a boss of the number 5 mine at the time, remembered that Chung, a good friend of Thomas and his wife, had gone to the mine to warn him after the riot began. Thomas had already gone home, but Chung, realizing that he was in danger, escaped to the surrounding hills, where he hid for a number of days without anything to eat or drink. When he was found, Thomas recalled, he "was in a half crazed condition, brought on through fright and starvation, together with exhaustion." He and the Thomases remained friends. When Thomas's wife died, Chung would visit her grave. By then he was "an old man, seated on the coping of my wife's grave; in his hand, a few fragrant flowers . . . his token of respect for her memory. His devotion touched us."

And when Chung himself died, Thomas placed flowers on his grave every Memorial Day, recalling the words of the Scottish poet Thomas Campbell: "To live in hearts we leave behind / Is not to die."

Afterword

FACES

Sara Teasdale

People that I meet and pass
  In the city's broken roar,
Faces that I lose so soon
  And have never found before,

Do you know how much you tell
  In the meeting of our eyes,
How ashamed I am, and sad
  To have pierced your poor disguise?

Secrets rushing without sound
  Crying from your hiding places —
Let me go, I cannot bear
  The sorrow of the passing faces.

— People in the restless street,
  Can it be, oh can it be
In the meeting of our eyes
  That you know as much of me?

QUOTATION SOURCES

1. The Man from Spirit Cave

"[She] insisted that I": S. M. Wheeler, "Rattlesnake Incentive," 1940, unpublished field notes, Wheeler Papers, Nevada State Museum, Carson City, Nev., p. 2.

"After much tedious work": Wheeler, p. 2.

"Oscar, a partially mummified": "Among the Rock Hunters," *Desert Magazine,* November 1940, p. 32.

2. Making Faces from the Past

"elderly man, not very tall": Karl A. Baer, "Johann Sebastian Bach (1685–1750) in Medical History," *Bulletin of the Medical Library Association* 39 (July 1951): p. 208.

3. Amoroleck's Ancestors

"cautiously attacked": E. P. Valentine, *Report of the Exploration of the Hayes' Creek Mound, Rockbridge County, Va.* (Richmond Valentine Museum, 1903), p. 3.

"more than one hundred skeletons": Valentine, p. 3.

"with their knees": Carlos Santos, "Faces of the Past," *Richmond Times-Dispatch,* October 5, 2000.

"beat out his brains": Captain John Smith, *The Generall Historie of Virginia, New England & the Summer Isles: Together with the True Travels, Adventures, and Observations, and a Sea Grammar,* vol. 1 (Glasgow: James MacLehose and Sons, 1907), p. 130.

"were a people come from": Smith, p. 131.

"came to collections of human bones": Bernard Shipp, *The Indian and Antiquities of America* (Philadelphia: Sherman, 1897), p. 268.

"bones nearest the surface": Shipp, p. 269.

"They were in wars": Santos, "Faces," p. C4.

"Caucasian, negro, Mongolian": An Act to Preserve Racial Integrity. www2.vcdh.virginia.edu/encounter/projects/monacans/Contemporary_Monacans/racial.html.

"It shall hereafter be": An Act to Preserve Racial Integrity.

"This is to give you": Peter Hardin, "Documentary Genocide: Families Surnames on Racial Hit List," *Richmond Times-Dispatch,* March 2000, www.nps.gov/jame/historyculture/upload/Documentary-Genocide.pdf.

"giving us the most": Hardin.

"they were no more": Samuel R. Cook, "The Monacan Indian Nation: Asserting Tribal Sovereignty in the Absence of Federal Recognition," *Wicazo Sa Review* 17 (Fall 2002): p. 98.

"When we were coming to school": Melanie D. Haimes-Bartolf, "The Social Construction of Trace and Monacan Education in Amherst County, Virginia, 1908–1965: Monacan Perspectives," *History of Education Quarterly* 47 (November 2007): p. 400.

4. A Stranded Sailor from France

"The shot hit": William C. Foster, ed., *The La Salle Expedition on the Mississippi River: The Journal of Henri Joutel, 1684–1687* (Austin: Texas State Historical Association, 1998), p. 199.

5. Pearl from Colonial New York

"the size of a large grapefruit": Nancy Davis, e-mail interview by author, November 2, 2010.

"each family had a cow": Anne MacVicar Grant, *Memoirs of an American Lady: With Sketches of Manners and Scenes in America as They Existed Previous to the Revolution,* New York: Dodd, Mead, 1901), p. 38.

"the Sum of two pounds": Joel Munsell, *Collections on the History of Albany, from Its Discovery to the Present Time, with Notices of Its Public Institutions, and Biographical Sketches of Citizens Deceased,* vol. 2 (Albany: J. Munsell, 1867), p. 266.

"removing skeletons": Quoted in Charles L. Fisher, *Draft Cultural Resources Survey Report for PIN 1753.58.121, Pearl Street Reconstruction Part I: Archaeological Mitigation Report, City of Albany, New York,* report to the New York State Department of Transportation, Albany, July 2004, New York State Museum, Albany, p. 55.

"for a box to contain skeletons": Fisher, p. 55.

"box of human bones": Fisher, p. 55.

"Burying a large Box": Fisher, p. 55.

"ditch and drain ye water": George R. Howell and Jonathan Tenney, eds., *History of the County of Albany, New York, from 1609 to 1886* (New York: W. W. Munsell, 1886), p. 503.

"the Dirtiest I ever Saw": Warren Johnson, "Journal of Warren Johnson," in *In Mohawk Country: Early Narratives About a Native People,* eds. Dean R. Snow, Charles T. Gehring, and William A. Starna, (Syracuse, N.Y.: Syracuse University Press, 1996), p. 269.

"to read in her closet": Grant, p. 164.

"while living in Albany": Nancy Davis, e-mail interview by author, July 20, 2011.

"Today we honor three persons": *A Celebration of Resurrection, Rite of Christian Burial,* funeral service booklet, May 15, 1999.

6. The Forgotten Burying Ground at Schuyler Flatts

"recognize that only half": Modern American Poetry, "at the cemetery, walnut grove plantation, south carolina, 1989," www.english.illinois.edu/maps/poets/a_f/clifton/cemetery.htm

"17 working horses": The original document is at the Albany Institute of Art, Albany.

"a universal genius who made canoes": Anne MacVicar Grant, *Memoirs of an American Lady: With Sketches of Manners and Scenes in America as They Existed Previous to the Revolution* (New York: Dodd, Mead, 1901), p. 141.

"I think I have never seen people so happy": Grant, p. 35.

"showed symptoms of degeneracy": Grant, p. 141.

"offered 'a likely negro'": Joel Munsell, *Collections on the History of Albany, from Its Discovery to the Present Time, with Notices of Its Public Institutions, and Biographical Sketches of Citizens Deceased,* vol. 2 (Albany: J. Munsell, 1867), p. 196.

"30 Dollars Reward": Albany Centinel, February 28, 1804.

"so happy in servitude": Grant, p.35.

"he would give her": Olive Gilbert, *Narrative of Sojourner Truth, A Northern Slave* (New York: published for the author, 1853), p. 39.

"'Ah!' she says, with emphasis": Gilbert, pp. 39–40.

7. A Mexican Soldier from San Jacinto

"While pursuing the Mexicans": Quoted in Gregg J. Dimmick, *Sea of Mud: The Retreat of the Mexican Army After San Jacinto, An Archaeological Investigation* (Austin: Texas State Historical Assocation, 2004), p. 10.

"the scattered remains of numerous": Lucy Audubon, ed., *The Life of John James Audubon, the Naturalist* (New York: G. P. Putnam & Son, 1869), p. 408.

"fifty-five Africans": Ann Fabian, *The Skull Collectors: Race, Science, and America's Unburied Dead* (Chicago: University of Chicago Press, 2010), p. 14.

"the Academy sent": Emily S. Renschler and Janet Monge, "The Samuel George Morton Cranial Collection: Historical Significance and New Research," *Expedition* 50, no. 3 (Winter 2008): p. 36.

"nose and midface were severely": Douglas Owsley, Richard Jantz, and Karin Bruwelheide, "Cranial Injuries in Six Mexican Soldiers Killed at San Jacinto" (paper presented at the Tenth Annual Battle of San Jacinto Symposium, Houston, April 1, 2010).

"not only do you get": Tori Brock, "Forensic Science, Archaeology Mix in Sam Houston Museum Exhibit," *Huntsville Item,* itemonline.com/local/x731682944/Forensic-science-archeology-mix-in-Sam-Houston-Museum-exhibit.

8. The People of the Almshouse Cemetery

"This woman is honest": Judy Patrick, "Era of the Almshouse Unfolds: Archaeologists Discover Remains of More Than 1,000 Poor," *Daily Gazette* (Schenectady, N.Y.), October 14, 2002, in "Almshouse Cemetery," webpage by Cliff Lamore, freepages.genealogy.rootsweb.ancestry.com/~clifflamere/Cem/CEM-AlbAlmshouse.htm.

"bohea tea sweetened with molasses": Joel Munsell, *The Annals of Albany,* vol. 10 (Albany: Munsell & Rowland, 1859), p. 234.

"1888 Mary Lammidge drowned" Poorhouse Story, "Albany Poorhouse Cemetery, Complete List (1880–1930)," www.poorhouse.story/NY_ALBANY_BurialList.htm.

"I have left [Mr.] Burley": Dulberger, p. 142.

"No, you can't": Dorothea L. Dix, "Memorial, to the Honorable the Legislature of the State of New York," in *Children and Youth in America: A Documentary History,* vol. 1, *1600–1865,* Robert H. Bremmer, ed. (Cambridge, Mass.: Harvard University Press, 1970), p. 775.

"several females chiefly in a state": Dix, pp. 775–76.

"totally dark and unventilated": Dix, p. 776.

"In the cell first opened was a madman": Dix, p. 776.

"brutalizing conditions of the most helpless": Dix, p. 776.

"chained to the beds": Dix, p. 777.

"1888 Mary Lammidge drowned" Poorhouse Story, "Albany Poorhouse Cemetery, Complete List (1880–1930)," www.poorhouse.story/NY_ALBANY_BurialList.htm.

"I have tried my best and cant": Judith A. Dulberger, *"Mother Donit fore the Best": Correspondence of a Nineteenth-Century Orphan Asylum* (Syracuse, N.Y.: Syracuse University Press, 1996), p. 140.

9. Thomas Smith, Buffalo Soldier

"murders, suicides, fatal accidents": Michael E. Ruane, "Old West Mystery, Solved in D.C.," *Washington Post,* June 16, 2009, www.washingtonpost.com/wp-dyn/content/article/2009/06/15/AR2009061503013.html.

"committed 'nuisances' in all": Marion Cox Grinstead, "Back at the Fort," in *Fort Craig: The United States Fort on the Camino Real,* eds. Charles Carroll and Lynne Sebastian (Socorro, N.M.: U.S. Department of the Interior, Bureau of Land Management, 2000), p. 54.

"often distinctly perceptible": John Shaw Billings, *A Report on Barracks and Hospitals, with Descriptions of Military Posts,* Circular No. 4, War Department, Surgeon General's Office (Washington, D.C.: Government Printing Office, 1870), p. 246.

"impurities in the air": Peggy A. Gerow, *Guardians of the Trail: Archaeological & Historical Investigations at Fort Craig* (Santa Fe,

N.M.: Bureau of Land Management, New Mexico State Office, 2004), p. 168.

"the weather on a daily basis": Gerow, p. 168.

"came up to the": Headquarters Department of the Missouri, *Proceedings of a General Court Martial Convened by Special Order No. 128,* July 11, 1877 (Washington, D.C.: National Archives QQ347), unnumbered.

"I did not know": *Proceedings.*

"I went to take": *Proceedings.*

10. Six Chinese Miners from Wyoming

"native-born Americans": Harvard University Library Open Collections Program, "Chinese Exclusion Act (1882)," "Immigration to the United States, 1789–1930," ocp.hul.harvard.edu/immigration/exclusion.html.

"the Chinese were responsible": Craig Storti, *Incident at Bitter Creek: The Story of the Rock Springs Chinese Massacre* (Ames: Iowa State University Press, 1991), p. 29.

"required all Chinese": Liping Zhu, "Ethnic Oasis: Chinese Immigrants in the Frontier Black Hills," in *Ethnic Oasis: The Chinese in the Black Hills,* Liping Zhu and Rose Estep Fosha, eds. (Pierre: South Dakota State Historical Society Press, 2004), p. 32.

"only 105 Chinese immigrants per year": Harvard Open Collections, "Chinese Exclusion Act."

"A fearful explosion took place": *Reno Evening Gazette,* March 7, 1881.

"an anti-Black, anti-Indian": A. Dudley Gardner, "Chinese Emigrants in Southwest Wyoming 1868–1885," in *Chinese on the American Frontier,* ed. Arif Dirlik (Lanham, Md.: Rowman and Littlefield, 2001), p. 341.

"planned to discharge": Gardner, p. 342.

"About 20 dead Chinamen": *Evening Gazette* (Port Jervis, New York), March 5, 1881.

"an afterworld suitcase": Laura J. Pasacreta, "White Tigers and Azure Dragons: Overseas Chinese Burial Practices in the Canadian and American West (1850s to 1910s)" (master's thesis, Simon Fraser University, 2005), p. 135.

"Whenever the mob met": History Matters: The U.S. Survey Course on the Web, "To This We Dissented: The Rock Springs Riot," historymatters.gmu.edu/d/5043/.

"The dead body of Leo Sun Tsung": History Matters.

"riding his horse": Yen Tzu-kuei, "Rock Springs Incident," in Dirlik, *Chinese on the American Frontier,* p. 358.

"was in a half crazed": David G. Thomas, "David G. Thomas' Memories of the Chinese Riot," as told to his daughter Mrs. J. H. Goodnough, in Dirlik, *Chinese on the American Frontier,* p. 354.

"an old man, seated": Thomas, p. 354.

SELECTED BIBLIOGRAPHY

I read many works and consulted many individuals as I researched this book. Here are the main sources I used, arranged by topic:

Spirit Cave Man

The best source of information about Spirit Cave Man is S. M. Wheeler's brief field notes, stored under lock and key at the Nevada State Museum. I was able to read the three pages of the notes in which Wheeler describes the discovery and excavation of Spirit Cave Man: "Rattlesnake Incentive," 1940, unpublished field notes, Wheeler Papers (Nevada State Museum, Carson City).

For more detailed, scientific information, the *Nevada Historical Society Quarterly* 40 (Spring 1997) issue, edited by Donald R. Tuohy and Amy Dansie, is devoted to the research studies on Spirit Cave Man. Among these valuable articles are Heather Joy Hecht Edgar, "Paleopathology of the Wizards Beach Man (AHUR 2023) and the Spirit Cave Mummy (AHUR 2064)" (pp. 57–61); B. Sunday Eiselt, "Fish Remains from the Spirit Cave Paleofecal Material: 9,400 Year Old Evidence for Great Basin Utilization of Small Fishes" (pp. 117–39); L. Kyle Napton, "The Spirit Cave Mummy: Coprolite Investigations" (pp. 97–104); S. M. Wheeler, "Cave Burials Near Fallon, Nevada" (pp. 15–17); and Peter E. Wigand, "Native American Diet and Environmental Contexts of the Holocene Revealed in the Pollen of Human Fecal Material" (pp. 105–16).

Popular accounts of Spirit Cave Man are few and usually found on only a few pages within a book. The best popular sources I found are Jeff Benedict, *No Bone Unturned: Inside the World of a Top Forensic Scientist and His Work on America's Most Notorious Crimes and Disasters* (New York: Perennial, 2004); Elaine Dewar, *Bones: Discovering the First Americans* (New York: Carroll and Graf, 2002); and Carey Goldberg, "Oldest Mummy 'Found' on Museum Shelf" (*New York Times,* April 27, 1996).

As for the controversy surrounding Spirit Cave Man, two excellent sources are Pat Barker, Cynthia Ellis, and Stephanie Damadio, *Determination of Cultural Affiliation of Ancient Human Remains from Spirit Cave, Nevada* (Reno, Nev.: Bureau of Land Management, 2000), and Heather J. H. Edgar, et al., "Contextual Issues in Paleoindian Repatriation: Spirit Cave Man as a Case Study" (*Journal of Social Archaeology* 7 [February 2007]: pp. 101–22).

Frank J. Mullen Jr., "Battle for the Bones" (*Reno Gazette Journal,* May 7, 2006), describes how Vivian Olds has taught her students about Spirit Cave Man.

David J. Meltzer, *First Peoples in a New World: Colonizing Ice Age America* (Berkeley: University of California Press, 2009), provided me with a comprehensive look at the theories surrounding the first immigrants to North America.

Finally, I spoke to Sharon Long at length regarding her work in reconstructing Spirit Cave Man's face. Douglas Owsley and Sharon Long, "Facial Reconstruction of One Late Prehistoric and Two Paleo-American Skulls from Nevada," unpublished report (May 1998), also gives pertinent information about Spirit Cave Man's bioarchaeological analysis and his facial reconstruction; Sharon Long provided me with her personal copy.

Facial Reconstruction

Anyone interested in the artistry and history of facial reconstruction should probably start where I did, by reading John Prag and Richard Neave, *Making Faces: Using Forensic and Archaeological Evidence* (London: British Museum Press, 1997). It provides an excellent summary of the history of facial reconstruction followed by numerous detailed compelling examples of historical reconstructions done by Neave, who is considered by many to be the most accomplished facial-reconstruction sculptor working today. Two other books that provide good background information are Caroline Wilkinson, *Forensic Facial Reconstruction* (Cambridge: Cambridge University Press, 2004), and Karen T. Taylor, *Forensic Art and Illustration* (Boca Raton, Fla.: CRC Press, 2001). Ian Wilson, *Past Lives: Unlocking the Secrets of Our Ancestors* (London: Cassell, 2001), offers an assortment of various historical facial reconstructions throughout the world.

For more detailed information about early facial reconstructions, I relied on Maria Luisa Azzaroli Puccetti, Libertso Perugi, and Paolo Scarini, "Gaetano Giulio Zumbo: The Founder of Anatomic Wax Modeling" (*Pathology Annual* 30 [1995]: pp. 169–281); E. Strouhal, "Five Plastered Skulls from Pre-Pottery Neolithic B Jericho, Anthropological Study," (*Paléorient* 1 [1973]: pp. 231–47); and Harris Hawthorne Wilder, "The Physiognomy of the Indians of Southern New England" (*American Anthropologist* 14 [July–September 1912]: pp. 415–36).

For the story of Bach's reconstruction, I found David Gaynor Yearsley, *Bach and the Meanings of Counterpoint* (Cambridge: Cambridge University Press, 2002), and Karl A. Baer, "Johann Sebastian Bach (1685–1750) in Medical History" (*Bulletin of the Medical Library Association* 39 [July 1951]: pp. 206–11), especially helpful.

Amoroleck's Ancestors

The best source of information about the Monacan Indian Nation today that I found is Karenne Wood and Diane Shields, *The Monacan Indians: Our Story* (Madison Heights, Va.: Monacan Indian Nation, n.d.), available at the Monacan Ancestral Museum.

To learn more about the history of the Monacans, including their mounds, I read David I. Bushnell Jr., "The Native Tribes of Virginia" (*Virginia Magazine of History and Biography* 30 [April 1922]: pp. 123–32); Andrew Cockburn, *Journey Through Hallowed Ground: Birthplace of the American Ideal* (Washington, D.C.: National Geographic, 2008); Samuel R. Cook, "The Monacan Indian Nation: Asserting Tribal Sovereignty in the Absence of Federal Recognition" (*Wicazo Sa Review* 17 [Fall 2002]: pp. 91–116; Debra L. Gold, *The Bioarchaeology of Virginia Burial Mounds* (Tuscaloosa: University of Alabama Press, 2004) and "Osteological Analysis of the Hayes Creek Mound (44RB 2), Rockbridge County, Virginia: Descriptive Report," unpublished report (Richmond: Virginia Department of Historic Resources, December 15, 1999); Jeffrey L. Hantman, "Between Powhatan and Quirank: Reconstructing Monacan Culture and History in the Context of Jamestown" (*American Anthropologist* 92 [September 1990]: pp. 676–90) and "Caliban's Own Voice: American Indian View of the Other in Colonial Virginia" (*New Literary History* 23 [1992]: pp. 69–81); Jeffrey L. Hantman, Karenne Wood, and Diane Shields, "Writing Collaborative History" (*Archaeology* 53 [September/October 2000]: pp. 56–59); Peter W. Houck and Mintcy D. Maxham, *Indian Island in Amherst County* (Lynchburg, Va.: Warwick House, 1993); E. P. Valentine, *Report of the Exploration of the Hayes' Creek Mound Rockbridge County, Va.* (Richmond: Valentine Museum, 1903), makes interesting reading as well and shows numerous photographs of the excavation of Hayes Creek.

For an excellent account of the problems that the Monacans faced in receiving an education in Virginia, I referred to Melanie D. Haimes-Bartolf, "The Social Construction of Race and Monacan Education in Amherst County, Virginia, 1908–1965: Monacan Perspectives" (*History of Education Quarterly* 47 [November 2007]: pp. 389–415).

For information about Walter Ashby Plecker's racist campaign against the Monacans and other Virginia Indian tribes, I found the following sources informative: Warren Fiske, "The Black-and-White World of Walter Ashby Plecker" (*Virginian-Pilot,* August 18, 2004, hamptonroads.com/2004/blackandwhite-world-walter-ashby-plecker); Peter Hardin, "Documentary Genocide: Families' Surnames on Racial Hit List" (*Richmond Times-Dispatch,* March 5, 2000, www.nps.gov/jame/historyculture/upload/Documentary-Genocide.pdf); W. A. Plecker, "Virginia's Attempt to Adjust the Color Problem (*American Journal of Public Health* 15 [1925]: pp. 111–15); and Philip Reilly, "The Virginia Racial Integrity Act Revisited: The Plecker-Laughlin Correspondence: 1928–1930" (*American Journal of Medical Genetics* 16 [1983]: pp. 483–92).

Rosemary Clark Whitlock, *The Monacan Indian Nation of Virginia: The Drums of Life* (Tuscaloosa: University of Alabama Press, 2008), contains oral histories of many Monacans and provides vivid accounts of their experiences with racism in Virginia.

I spoke with Sharon Long many times about her reconstructions of the Monacans. I also relied on Carlos Santos, "Faces of the Past" (*Richmond-Times Dispatch,* October 5, 2000), for information about the reconstructions and his "Monacan Remains Reinterred: Forebears Remembered in Traditional Ceremony (*Richmond-Times Dispatch,* October 9, 2000), for the details surrounding the burial of the remains from the Hayes Creek mound.

Finally, I also conducted extensive and extremely helpful e-mail interviews with Jeffrey Hantman, archaeology professor at the University of Virginia, who is considered an expert on the history of the Monacan Indian Nation; Catherine Slusser, an archaeologist and Richmond deputy director of Virginia's Department of Historic Resources; and Karenne Wood, a member of the Monacan Indian Nation and director of the Virginia Indian Heritage Program at the Virginia Foundation for the Humanities.

La Belle Sailor

The most complete account of the history and discovery of *La Belle* is James E. Bruseth and Toni S. Turner, *From a Watery Grave: The Discovery and Excavation of La Salle's Shipwreck,* La Belle (College Station: Texas A&M University Press, 2005). More details about the initial discovery are provided in J. Barto Arnold III, "The Texas Historical Commission's Underwater Archaeological Survey of 1995 and the Preliminary Report on the *Belle,* La Salle's Shipwreck of 1686" (*Historical Archaeology* 30, no. 4 [1996]: pp. 66–87), and Stephen Harrigan, "In Search of La Salle" (*Texas Monthly*, January 1979: pp. 88–90).

For historical information about La Salle and his attempt to establish a Louisiana colony, I read William C. Foster, ed., *The La Salle Expedition on the Mississippi River: The Journal of Henri Joutel, 1684–1687* (Austin: Texas State Historical Association, 1998); Francis Parkman's classic *La Salle and the Discovery of the Great West* (New York: Signet, 1963); Robert S. Weddle, *The Wreck of the* Belle, *the Ruin of La Salle* (College Station: Texas A&M University Press, 2001); and Robert S. Weddle, Mary Christian Morkovsky, and Patricia Galloway, eds., *La Salle, the Mississippi, and the Gulf: Three Primary Documents,* trans. Ann Linda Bell and Robert S. Weddle (College Station: Texas A&M University Press, 1987).

I also interviewed J. Barto Arnold III about his discovery of *La Belle* and learned a great deal about the magnetometer and the events on the morning of the discovery.

Pearl from Colonial Albany

One of my own research highlights from this book was becoming acquainted with Albany's rich and varied history. In particular, I found Charles L. Fisher, *People, Places, and Material Things: Historical Archaeology of Albany, New York,* New York State Museum Bulletin 499 (Albany: New York State Education Department, 2003), quite fascinating, with its various articles about the Pearl Street and other Albany excavations. Among the most useful were Nancy Davis, "The Cultural Landscape at the Site of the Lutheran Church Lot and Burial Ground" (pp. 71–81) and Shawn Phillips, "Skeletal Analysis of the Human Remains from the Lutheran Church Lot, 1670–1816" (pp. 57–62). I also enjoyed Charles L. Fisher, et al., "Privies and Parasites: The Archaeology of Health Conditions in Albany, New York" (*Historical Archaeology* 41, no. 4: pp. 172–97), and Charles L. Fisher, *Draft Cultural Resources Survey Report for PIN 1753.58.121, Pearl Street Reconstruction Part I: Archaeological Mitigation Report, City of Albany, New York,* Report to the New York State Department of Transportation (Albany: New York State Museum, July 2004).

For a nonarchaeological look at Albany's past, I used George R. Howell and Jonathan Tenney, eds., *History of the County of Albany, New York, from 1609 to 1886* (New York: W. W. Munsell, 1886); Joel Munsell, *The Annals of Albany*, vol. 1, 2d. edition (Albany: Joel Munsell, 1869), and *Collections on the History of Albany, from Its Discovery to the Present Time, with Notices of Its Public Institutions, and Biographical Sketches of Citizens Deceased*, vol. 2 (Albany: Joel Munsell, 1867); and Dean R. Snow, Charles T. Gehring, and William A. Starna, eds., *In Mohawk Country: Early Narratives About a Native People* (Syracuse, N.Y.: Syracuse University Press, 1996).

Other books I consulted about the history of Albany were David G. Hackett, *The Rude Hand of Innovation: Religion and Social Order in Albany, New York 1652–1836* (New York: Oxford University Press, 1991) and Donna Merwick, *Possessing Albany, 1630–1710: The Dutch and English Experiences* (New York: Cambridge University Press, 1990).

I also wrote frequent e-mails filled with questions (and sometimes questionable assumptions) to Nancy Davis, an archaeologist at the New York State Museum in Albany, who wrote helpful volumes in clarifying my account. The sculptor Gay Malin also answered repeated e-mail questions to guide me through the reconstruction process. To learn more about Gay Malin's work at the New York State Museum, the best source is on DVD and available at the NYSM: *The Science and Art of the Facial Reconstruction Process,* Software Series No. 4. (Albany: New York State Department of Education, n.d.).

The final funeral service for Pearl was contained in *A Celebration of the Resurrection—Rite of Christian Burial* (May 15, 1999, Albany, N.Y.). Nancy Davis was kind enough to share her copy with me.

Schuyler Flatts Enslaved Workers

Little has been written about the Schuyler Flatts burying ground. The main sources of information are Lisa Anderson, "Schuyler Flatts Burial Ground Report," unpublished report (Albany: New York State Museum); Lisa Anderson, Vanessa Newell Dale, and Dawn M. Lawrence, "Life, Work, and Death Among 18th Century African Americans in Rural Upstate New York (paper presented at the forty-sixth annual meeting of the Northeast Anthropological Association in an organized symposium entitled "Bioarchaeology of the Disenfranchised," May 2006 (cdbhba.files.wordpress.com/2008/06/may-2006-nys-museum-report-on-life-work-and-death-among-18th-century-african-americans-in-rural-upstate-new-york.pdf); Hartgen Archaeological Associates, *Phase III Archaeological Site Mitigation Data Retrieval Field Excavation Report*, April

2007 (cdbhba.files.wordpress.com/2008/06/april-2007-phase-iii-archeologicalsite-migiation-data-retrieval-field-excavation-report.pdf); and Esther J. Lee et al., "MtDNA Origins of an Enslaved Labor Force from the 18th Century Schuyler Flatts Burial Ground in Colonial Albany, NY: Africans, Native Americans, and Malagasy" (*Journal of Archaeological Science* 36 [2009]: pp. 2805–10).

For information about slavery in New York, I consulted Edgar J. McManus, *A History of Negro Slavery in New York* (Syracuse, N.Y.: Syracuse University Press, 1970), Janny Venema, Beverwijck: A Dutch Village on the American Frontier (Albany: State University of New York Press, 2003).

Joyce Hansen and Gary McGowan, *Breaking Ground, Breaking Silence: The Story of New York's African Burial Ground* (New York: Henry Holt, 1998), and Marilyn Yalom and Reid S. Yalom, *The American Resting Place: 400 Years of History Through Our Cemeteries and Burial Grounds* (Boston: Houghton Mifflin, 2008), were helpful in providing me a context for African burying grounds in the United States.

For primary-source material, I used Anne MacVicar Grant, *Memoirs of an American Lady: With Sketches of Manners and Scenes in America as They Existed Previous to the Revolution* (New York: Dodd, Mead, 1901), and Joel Munsell, *Collections on the History of Albany, from Its Discovery to the Present Time, with Notices of Its Public Institutions, and Biographical Sketches of Citizens Deceased,* vol. 2 (Albany: J. Munsell, 1867).

Finally, I corresponded with Lisa Anderson, bioarchaeologist at the New York State Museum, with many questions about the analysis of the burials.

Mexican Soldier from San Jacinto

The only historical and scientific accounts to date regarding the four Mexican soldiers whose skulls were recovered at the San Jacinto Battleground are Jeffrey D. Dunn, "The Mexican Soldier Skulls of San Jacinto Battleground," and Douglas Owsley, Richard Jantz, and Karin Bruwelheide, "Cranial Injuries in Six Mexican Soldiers Killed at San Jacinto," both papers presented at the Tenth Annual Battle of San Jacinto Symposium (Houston, April 1, 2010). Both can be retrieved online at the San Jacinto Battleground Conservancy website (www.friendsofsanjacinto.com/articles/mexican-soldier-skulls-san-jacinto-battleground).

Ann Fabian, *The Skull Collectors: Race, Science, and America's Unburied Dead* (Chicago: University of Chicago Press, 2010), and Emily S. Renschler and Janet Monge, "The Samuel George Morton Cranial Collection: Historical Significance and New Research" (*Expedition* 50, no. 3: pp. 30–38) offer a thorough look at Samuel George Morton's cranial collection. Lucy Audubon, *The Life of John James Audubon, the Naturalist* (New York: G. P. Putnam & Son, 1869), includes Audubon's journals from the Texas trip in which he collected the four skulls.

For background information on the Texas War for Independence, I relied on H. W. Brands, *Lone Star Nation: The Epic Story of the Battle for Texas Independence* (New York: Anchor Books, 2004); Gregg J. Dimmick, *Sea of Mud: The Retreat of the Mexican Army After San Jacinto, An Archaeological Investigation* (Austin: Texas State Historical Association, 2004); Stephen L. Hardin, *Texian Illiad: A Military History of the Texas Revolution* (Austin: University of Texas Press, 1994); and Alan C. Huffines, *The Texas War of Independence 1835–1836: From Outbreak to the Alamo to San Jacinto* (Oxford: Osprey Publishing, 2005).

Tori Brock, "Forensic Science, Archaeology Mix in Sam Houston Museum Exhibit" (*Huntsville Item*, April 11, 2011, itemonline.com/local/x731682944/Forensic-science-archeology-mix-in-Sam-Houston-Museum-exhibit), includes an interview with the sculptor Amanda Danning.

I spoke with Amanda Danning many times, sometimes as she was reconstructing the face of the Mexican soldier, to gather more information about her work and the injuries that the soldier sustained.

People of the Albany Almshouse

The two most comprehensive published sources about the excavations at the almshouse cemetery are both by Martin C. Solano: "Gone but Not Forgotten: Life and Death in the Albany County Almshouse" (*The Dutch Settlers Society of Albany Yearbook* 54 [2001–5]: pp. 43–58) and "The Life Stresses of Poverty: Skeletal and Historical Indicators of Activity Patterns in the Albany County Almshouse Skeletal Collection, 1825–1925" (Ph.D. dissertation, State University of New York–Albany, 2006). Judy Patrick, "Era of the Almshouse Unfolds: Archaeologists Discover Remains of More Than 1,000 Poor" (*Daily Gazette,* Schenectady, N.Y., October 14, 2002, in "Almshouse Cemetery," webpage by Cliff Lamere, freepages.genealogy.rootsweb.ancestry.com/~clifflamere/Cem/CEM-AlbAlmshouse.htm), is another enlightening source about the almshouse excavations. For a bureaucratic (and yet equally personal) look at the burials in the almshouse cemetery, I used Poorhouse Story, "Albany Poorhouse Cemetery, Complete List (1880–1930)," www.poorhousestory.com/NY_ALBANY_BurialList.htm.

For historical background on the Albany almshouse, I read Reginald Byron, *Irish America* (New York: Oxford University Press, 1999); Dorothea L. Dix, "Memorial, to the Honorable the Legislature of the State of New York," in *Children and Youth in America: A Documentary History*, vol. 1: *1600–1865,* ed. Robert H. Bremmer (Cambridge, Mass.: Harvard University Press, 1970); Judith A. Dulberger, *Mother Donit fore the Best: Correspondence of a Nineteenth-Century Orphan Asylum* (Syracuse, N.Y.: Syracuse University Press, 1996); George Rogers Howell, *Bi-centennial History of County of Albany, 1609–1886,* vol. 2 (New York: W. W. Munsell, 1886); and Joel Munsell, *The Annals of Albany,* vol. 10 (Albany, N.Y.: Joel Munsell, 1859).

For a better understanding of the use of almshouses in the

United States I found Michael B. Katz, *In the Shadow of the Poorhouse: A Social History of Welfare in America* (New York: Basic Books, 1996), helpful.

I also had many e-mail conversations with the archaeologist Andrea Lain of the New York State Museum regarding the burials and their excavations.

Buffalo Soldier Thomas Smith

For information about the looting of Fort Craig's cemetery, I read Samir S. Patel, "The Case of the Missing Buffalo Soldier" (*Archaeology,* March/April 2009: pp. 40–44); Michael E. Ruane, "Old West Mystery, Solved in D.C." (*Washington Post,* June 16, 2009, www.washingtonpost.com/wp-dyn/content/article/2009/06/15/AR2009061503013.html), and "Smithsonian Unearths Buffalo Soldier's Story: Student Helps Solve Mystery of Looted Frontier Trooper's Skull" (*Washington Post,* June 17, 2009).

The most detailed sources about Thomas Smith and Levi Morris, however, were unpublished papers and reports that were kindly provided to me. These included Alaina Goff, "Report of the Skeletal Remains Excavated at the Fort Craig Post Cemetery"; Jeffrey Hanson, "Looting of the Fort Craig Cemetery: Damage Done and Lessons Learned"; Jeffrey Hanson and Mark Hungerford, "Righting History: Fort Craig Cemetery and the Buffalo Soldiers"; and Mark A. Hungerford, "Fort Craig Cemetery Report."

To learn more about Fort Craig, I relied on John Shaw Billings, *A Report on Barracks and Hospitals, with Descriptions of Military Posts,* Circular No. 4 (War Department, Surgeon General's Office,Washington, D.C.: Government Printing Office, 1870); Peggy A. Gerow, *Guardians of the Trail: Archaeological and Historical Investigations at Fort Craig* (Santa Fe: Bureau of Land Management, New Mexico State Office, 2004); and Marion Cox Grinstead, "Back at the Fort," in *Fort Craig: The United States Fort on the Camino Real,* ed. Charles Carroll and Lynne Sebastian (Socorro, N.M.: U.S. Department of the Interior, Bureau of Land Management, 2000), pp. 27–63.

Monroe Lee Billington, *New Mexico's Buffalo Soldiers 1866–1900* (Niwot: University Press of Colorado, 1991); Ron Field and Alexander Bielakowski, *Buffalo Soldiers: African American Troops in the U.S. Forces 1866–1945* (Oxford: Osprey Publishing, 2008); William H. Leckie, *The Buffalo Soldiers: A Narrative of the Negro Cavalry in the West* (Norman: University of Oklahoma Press, 1967); Elizabeth D. Leonard, *Men of Color to Arms! Black Soldiers, Indian Wars, and the Quest for Equality* (New York: W. W. Norton, 2010); and Frank N. Schubert, *Voices of the Buffalo Soldier: Records, Reports, and Recollections of Military Life and Service in the West* (Albuquerque: University of New Mexico Press, 2003), were invaluable sources of information about the buffalo soldiers.

I also had many conversations with Amanda Danning about her work on the reconstructions of Thomas Smith and Levi Morris. And her husband, James Brasher, shared his own research on Thomas Smith and Levi Morris, including the court-martial proceedings of Peter Johnson, the soldier who killed Private Morris.

Six Chinese Miners

Information about the six Chinese burials is published in two main sources: Rennie Phillips, "A More Complete Picture of Chinese Life on the Wyoming Frontier" (plan B paper, University of Wyoming, 1999); and Rennie Phillips Polidora, "Six Historic Chinese Burials from Southwestern Wyoming," in *Skeletal Biology and Bioarchaeology of the Northwestern Plains,* ed. George W. Gill and Rick L. Weathermon (Salt Lake City: University of Utah Press, 2008: pp. 94–103). Laura J. Pasacreta, "White Tigers and Azure Dragons: Overseas Chinese Burial Practices in the Canadian and American West (1850s to 1910s)" (master's thesis, Simon Fraser University, 2005), also mentions the six burials and provides a great deal of information about Chinese-immigrant burials in western North America.

One of the best general books about Chinese immigrants in the western United States is Arif Dirlik, ed., *Chinese on the American Frontier* (Lanham, Md.: Rowman and Littlefield, 2001). This book contains three articles relevant to the Wyoming burials: A. Dudley Gardner, "Chinese Emigrants in Southwest Wyoming 1868–1885" (pp. 341–48); David G. Thomas, "David G. Thomas' Memories of the Chinese Riot," as told to his daughter Mrs. J. H. Goodnough (pp. 349–54); and Yen Tzu-kuei, "Rock Springs Incident" (pp. 355–65).

Liping Zhu, *A Chinaman's Chance: The Chinese on the Rocky Mountain Mining Frontier* (Boulder: University Press of Colorado, 1997), and Liping Zhu, "Ethnic Oasis: Chinese Immigrants in the Frontier Black Hills," in *Ethnic Oasis: The Chinese in the Black Hills,* ed. Liping Zhu and Rose Estep Fosha (Pierre: South Dakota State Historical Society Press, 2004, pp. 3–43), supplied me with an understanding of the struggles and successes of Chinese immigrants on the western frontier. Harvard University Library Open Collections Program, "Chinese Exclusion Act (1882)," "Immigration to the United States, 1789–1930" (ocp.hul.harvard.edu/immigration/exclusion.html), gives a basic summary of the Chinese Exclusion Act and links to other sources on the topic.

To learn more about the Rock Springs massacre, I read Paul Crane and Alfred Larson, "The Chinese Massacre" (Part 1: *Annals of Wyoming* 12 [January 1940]: pp. 47–55; Part 2: *Annals of Wyoming* 12 [April 1940]: pp. 153–61); History Matters: The U.S. Survey Course on the Web, "To This We Dissented: The Rock Springs Riot" (historymatters.gmu.edu/d/5043/); and Craig Storti, *Incident at Bitter Creek: The Story of the Rock Springs Chinese Massacre* (Ames: Iowa State University Press, 1991).

Finally, the University of Wyoming professors Rick Weathermon and George Gill answered many questions both in person and by e-mail about the burials, and Rennie Phillips Polidora, who took time from her law school courses, did the same.

ACKNOWLEDGMENTS

Although I didn't realize it at first, researching this book ended up being a journey that took me more than 60,000 miles.

My search for information began in Scotland in November 2009 and ended in Texas in August 2011, with many stops and repeat visits along the way. I climbed a rocky hill to an ancient cave, explored the back rooms of museums, observed sculptors at work, interviewed archaeologists and anthropologists, visited cemeteries right before the gates would be locked at sunset, hunted in library archives for just the right historic photographs, handled human bones, searched for old books, photographed everything I could—and made many new friends.

At the start, once I knew that I was writing a book about the facial reconstruction of historic remains, I still had no idea what geographic direction this book would take. To make that decision, I traveled to Dundee, Scotland, and Nij-megen, Netherlands, to interview two of the world's foremost authorities on facial reconstruction: Caroline Wilkinson and Richard Neave, who have both written books on the subject.

In Dundee I spent a few hours talking with Professor Wilkinson, first over coffee in a small cafeteria and then in her reconstruction lab at the University of Dundee. Her thoughtful answers educated me about the main issues in the field. A few weeks later, in Nijmegen, I joined Professor Neave for a long, question-filled breakfast, then watched him reconstruct the face of a man over the next two days. As he worked, he answered my questions about his technique and the challenges he faced in some of his earlier historic reconstructions.

At that early stage in my research, I entertained the possibility of writing a book that was more global. But after speaking to these experts and exploring more, I chose in the end to focus on the facial reconstructions of historical remains found in North America. Though the contributions of Professors Wilkinson and Neave are not apparent, the book would not have been the same without their initial contributions. I am honored that I had a chance to meet them and learn from them both.

The search for facial-reconstruction artists in North America led me to Nevada, Wyoming, Texas, New Mexico, and New York—and to three superb and very talented sculptors: Sharon Long, Amanda Danning, and Gay Malin. This book would not have been possible without their willingness to educate me (no matter how long it took me to learn) and their generosity in sharing photographs of their work.

Sharon Long welcomed me to her home on short notice and supplied me with a stack of newspaper clippings, books, photographs, and slides about Spirit Cave Man and her reconstruction of him. As with many of my contacts, we had only a few hours to talk the first time we met. We managed not only to cover everything but to make time for dinner at a local Mexican restaurant. By the time I left, she had also told me about her Monacan reconstructions and introduced me to Professor George Gill, who told me about the six Chinese burials in the Human Remains Repository.

Amanda Danning also greeted me in her Texas home for a few hours one afternoon to talk about her reconstruction of buffalo soldier Thomas Smith. She showed me samples of her other work and told me about upcoming reconstructions. In the end I was fortunate to be able to watch her reconstruct the faces of the Mexican soldier at the annual San Jacinto symposium in Houston in 2010 and of the French sailor in her sculpting studio in August 2011.

Gay Malin and I first met over lunch for a few hours on a cold February afternoon in Albany. The archaeologist Andrea Lain had arranged the meeting so that the three of us could talk about Gay's almshouse reconstructions. In no time at all, though, I learned about her other reconstructions: Pearl and the people from the Schuyler Flatts burying ground. Then Andrea and Gay took me back to the museum for a quick tour, not only of her facial reconstructions but of some of the incredible exhibits that she helped create there.

From these relatively short initial meetings, the book grew from three possible reconstructions into nine. All I can say to these three women is thank you for allowing me to share your work with others. I enjoyed every second of working with you. What an amazing talent you have for bringing history to life!

As I researched and wrote each chapter, I relied on many people to provide information or images. Most people I approached were very generous with their time and knowledge; only a few refused to assist in any way. I want to thank everyone who helped as well as those who did not. When people share their work and often a lifetime of experience with me, I know they have trusted me to tell the story correctly; it is a huge honor. Even when someone refuses to provide information, the challenge of finding it another way is often more personally rewarding for me. Both groups helped make this book what it is.

I owe special thanks to the following people, arranged by subject:

Spirit Cave Man. To Vivian Olds, a dedicated teacher from Fernley, Nevada, I offer a huge thank you! I had read about Vivian's attempts to teach her students about Spirit Cave Man. After I e-mailed her, she not only invited me into her Fernley classroom to talk to her students, but she gave me a personal tour of Spirit Cave (twice) and the nearby sites of Stillwater Marsh and Grimes Point. She also helped arrange my visit with Don Tuohy, an anthropologist who studied the remains of Spirit Cave Man during his career at the Nevada State Museum. Donnelyn Curtis of the University of Nevada at Reno's Special Collections was also instrumental in helping me add an archival photograph of Spirit Cave Man to the book.

The Monacans. Three wonderful and personable scholars guided me with this chapter. Jeffrey Hantman of the University of Virginia and Catherine Slusser with the Virginia Department of Historic Resources (DHR) answered my many queries about the Monacans and their burial mounds via e-mail; Catherine also supplied a number of DHR reports that helped give me a better foundation in understanding the Monacan remains and their repatriation.

My largest dept of gratitude goes to Karenne Wood, the historic officer of the Monacan Indian Nation, who corresponded with me for more than a year. We met finally at the Monacan Ancestral Museum on the first day of the 2011 Monacan Nation Powwow. Karenne took me to Bear Mountain to see the cemetery of her ancestors, and we spent the better part of the morning talking. It was an unforgettable experience.

I also want to thank the photographer John Boal, who allowed me to use two of his wonderful Monacan portraits in the book.

The Sailor from *La Belle*. Barto Arnold of the Institute of Nautical Archaeology spoke to me at length about his role in the discovery of *La Belle* on the muddy bottom of Matagorda Bay. James Bruseth of the Texas Historic Commission was helpful in providing photographs to illustrate the excavation. And Amanda Danning deserves another shout-out, for pursuing the reconstruction of the French sailor Barange, even after the first replica skull was somehow mysteriously smashed (and not by her).

Pearl from Colonial Albany. Nancy Davis, a true gem of an archaeologist with the New York State Museum, wrote me lengthy e-mails explaining in detail everything that happened at the corner of Pearl and Howard Streets. She also read and reread my chapter on Pearl; the final version wouldn't have been the same without her help. Ralph Rataul of the New York State Museum helped gather photographs and worked hard to find the missing ones; the three chapters dealing with Albany benefitted enormously from his help.

The Schuyler Flatts Burying Ground. Lisa Anderson, bioarchaeologist from the New York State Museum, provided much of the research about the burials. Her work was invaluable to me, as were her suggestions for appropriate images. I want to thank her for this and for kindly reading and commenting on the chapter. Similarly, Corey McQuinn of Hartgen Archaeological Associates, an Albany firm responsible for the excavation of the burials, helped me locate photographs of the excavation, and the Town of Colonie granted permission to use them in the book. I am grateful to both for their contributions.

The San Jacinto Soldier. Jeff Dunn and Jan DeVault, the cofounders of the San Jacinto Battleground Conservancy, offered their help on this chapter. Jeff's research paved the way for Amanda Danning's reconstruction of Skull 556. Without him, there would be no chapter about the Mexican soldiers in this book. Janet Monge of the University of Pennsylvania and the keeper of the Morton Cranial Collection was instrumental in helping me obtain two photos to use in the chapter, and I thank her for this. Maureen Goldsmith at the Penn Museum photo archives was instrumental in getting images of the Morton Cranial Collection.

The Almshouse Burials. Andrea Lain, archaeologist with the New York State Museum, was part of the team that excavated the almshouse burials. She provided a great deal of information about the excavations and kindly read the chapter to offer suggestions. She was also my first contact at the museum; without her help, I would never have met Lisa Anderson and Nancy Davis—or Gay Malin. I also want to thank Tom Walsh, chief administrative office of the Parsons Child and Family Center in Albany, who helped me track down a few unforgettable photographs from the Albany Orphanage Asylum.

The Buffalo Soldiers. Mark Hungerford of the Albuquerque office of the Bureau of Reclamation provided much of the background information missing from published reports of the looting of Fort Craig. Jan Vaughn, a host at Fort Craig during the hot summer months, extended an important kindness to me. And Jim Brasher, whose serious interest in history led to some excellent research on Thomas Smith and Levi Morris, shared his invaluable discoveries with me.

The Six Chinese Miners. At dinner with Sharon Long and the anthropologist George Gill in Laramie, Wyoming, I learned about the six Chinese miners. Even though their faces had not been reconstructed, I heard the kernel of a story worth telling. For this and for the other information he provided, I thank Professor Gill. I also wish to thank Rennie Polidora, who studied the remains as a student of Professor Gill. Finally, I am indebted to Rick Weathermon, archaeologist and director of the Human Remains Repository at the University of Wyoming. He gave me a tour of the repository and allowed me to take photographs of it and the remains that are now in chapter 10. But I wouldn't have heard this story if it hadn't been for Sharon Long; another heartfelt thanks to her.

As my journey ended, I was struck by how many of the people I have mentioned above truly cared about the human remains that were found and felt a kindred bond with the people who had been discovered. I hope you share this sense of kinship, too.

My last thank-you has been reserved for my editor, Erica Zappy, for allowing me—very patiently—to make this meandering journey (no matter how many missed deadlines it took).

FOR FURTHER RESEARCH AND INFORMATION

Books

Spirit Cave Man: Patricia Lauber. *Who Came First? New Clues to Prehistoric Americans.* Washington, D.C.: National Geographic, 2003.

The Monacans. Keith Egloff and Deborah Woodward. *First People: The Early Indians of Virginia.* 2nd ed. Charlottesville: University of Virginia Press, 2006.

***La Belle* Sailor.** Mark G. Mitchell. *Raising* La Belle. Austin, Tex.: Eakin Press, 2002.

Schuyler Flatts. Joyce Hansen. *Breaking Ground, Breaking Silence: The Story of New York's African Burial Ground.* New York: Henry Holt, 1998.

The Almshouse Burials. Penny Colman. *Breaking the Chains: The Crusades of Dorothea Lynde Dix.* Lincoln, Neb.: ASJA Press, 2007.

Catherine Reef. *Alone in the World: Orphans and Orphanages in America.* New York: Clarion, 2005.

Museums

Monacan Indians

Monacan Indian Nation Ancestral Museum, 2009 Kenmore Rd., Amherst, VA

***La Belle* Shipwreck**

Seven Texas museums display artifacts from *La Belle*; each tells a different part of its story.

Calhoun County Museum, 301 S. Ann St., Port Lavaca, TX

Corpus Christi Museum of Science and History, 1900 N. Chaparral St., Corpus Christi, TX

La Petite Belle Homeport and Palacios Area Historical Museum, Commerce St., Palacios, TX

Matagorda County Museum, 2100 Ave. F, Bay City, TX

Museum of the Coastal Bend, Victoria College, 2200 E. Red River, Victoria, TX

Texana Museum, 403 N. Wells St., Edna, TX

Texas Maritime Museum, 1202 Navigation Circle, Rockport, TX

Colonial Albany and Almshouse Burials

New York State Museum, 222 Madison St., Albany, NY

African Burying Ground

African Burial Ground National Monument, 290 Broadway, New York, NY

Battle of San Jacinto

San Jacinto Museum of History, 1 Monument Circle, La Porte, TX

Almshouse History

Green County Historical Society Museum (former County Poor Farm), 918 Rolling Meadows Rd., Waynesburg, PA

Tenement Museum, 108 Orchard St., New York, NY

Buffalo Soldiers

Buffalo Soldiers National Museum, 1834 Southmore Blvd., Houston, TX

Fort Craig, 35 miles south of Socorro, NM

Chinese Immigrants

Chinese American Museum, 425 N. Los Angeles St., Los Angeles, CA

Chinese-America Museum of Chicago, 238 W. 23rd Street, Chicago, IL

Chinese Historical Society of America, 965 Clay St., San Francisco, CA

Museum of Chinese in America, 215 Centre St., New York, NY

Websites

Spirit Cave Man

The Spirit Cave Man Lawsuit: www.friendsofpast.org/spirit-cave.

Under One Sky: museums.nevadaculture.org/new_exhibits/cc-UnderOneSky/spiritcave.htm.

Monacan Indians

Jefferson's Excavation of an Indian Burial Mound: www.monticello.org/site/ research-and-collections/jeffersons-excavation-indian-burial-mound.

Monacan Indian Nation: www.monacannation.com.

Racial Integrity Act of 1924: www2.vcdh.virginia.edu/encounter/projects/monacans/Contemporary_Monacans/racial.html.

Virginia's First People, Past and Present: virginiaindians.pwnet.org/today/monacan.php.

La Belle

La Belle Shipwreck: www.texasbeyondhistory.net/belle.

La Salle Shipwreck Project: www.thc.state.tx.us/belle.

Modeling *La Belle*: Ship and Rig: nautarch.tamu.edu/model/report1/bellehull.htm.

Colonial Albany

Colonial Albany Project Website: www.nysm.nysed.gov/albany/welcome.html.

Schuyler Flatts Burial Ground

African Burial Ground: www.africanburialground.gov/ABG_Main.htm.

African Burial Ground National Monument: www.nps.gov/afbg/index.htm.

Sojourner Truth: www.sojournertruth.org.

Town of Colonie, Schuyler Flatts Cultural Park: www.colonie.org/historian/historical/schuyler.htm.

Battle of San Jacinto

Sons of Dewitt Colony Texas, Battle of San Jacinto: www.tamu.edu/faculty/ccbn/dewitt/batsanjacinto.htm.

Texas State Library and Archives Commission, Battle of San Jacinto: www.tsl.state.tx.us/treasures/republic/san-jacinto.html.

Albany Almshouse

Burial List of Albany Almshouse Cemetery, 1880–1930: www.poorhousestory. com/NY_ALBANY_BurialList.htm.

Poorhouse History of Albany County: www.poorhousestory.com/ALBANY.htm.

Buffalo Soldiers

Buffalo Soldiers and Indian Wars: www.buffalosoldier.net.

Chinese Immigrants

Angel Island Association, History: angelisland.org/history.

Central Pacific Railroad Photographic History Museum, Chinese-American Contribution to Transcontinental Railroad: cprr.org/Museum/Chinese.html.

Herbert Hoover Presidential Library and Museum, Chinese Americans: www.hoover.archives.gov/exhibits/China/Chinese_Americans/index.html.

ILLUSTRATION CREDITS

ii New York State Museum
vi James M. Deem
2–3, 5, 6, 7 James M. Deem
8 (top) YAY! DESIGN, based on a drawing in the unpublished field notes of Sidney Wheeler, 1940, Wheeler Papers (Nevada State Museum, Carson City)
(bottom) James M. Deem
9 Special Collections, Universityc of Nevada–Reno Library, UNRS-P2008-22-1
10 Sharon A. Long
13 (top) Mark Adams, with the permission of Sharon A. Long
(bottom left and right) Sharon A. Long
14–15 Getty Images/Hulton Archive
16 Getty Images/Neolithic
17 (top) Private collection
(bottom) Bridgeman Art Library
18, 19, 20 Private collection
21 (top left, top right, bottom left) Sharon A. Long
(bottom right) Reconstruction by Sharon A. Long; photograph by Chip Clark, National Museum of Natural History, Smithsonian Institution
22, 23 Reconstruction by Sharon A. Long; photographs by Chip Clark, National Museum of Natural History, Smithsonian Institution
24 (left) Getty Images/Alfred Eisenstaedt
(right) Library of Congress, USZ62-136583.
25 Vivian Olds
26 James M. Deem
28–29, 31 Valentine Richmond History Center
32 Private collection
33, 34 James M. Deem
36, 37 Photographs by Teri Miera, Sparks, Nevada, with the permission of Sharon A. Long
38 John Boal, johnboalphotography.com
39 James M. Deem
40, 41 Jackson Davis Collection, Special Collections, University of Virginia Library
42 James M. Deem
44–45 Private collection
47 James M. Deem
48, 49 Private collection
51, 52, 53 Texas Historical Commission
54 (top) AP Photo/Pat Sullivan
(bottom) Robert Clark/INSTITUTE
55 Texas Historical Commission
56 James M. Deem
57 (top, bottom left, and bottom center) James M. Deem
(bottom right) Amanda Danning
58, 59 James M. Deem
60–61 New York State Museum
62 James M. Deem
63 New York State Museum
64 Private collection
65, 66, 67 New York State Museum
68 Private collection
69 (top) New York State Museum
(bottom) Times Union, Albany, New York
70, 71 New York State Museum
72–73 Library of Congress, Historic American Buildings Survey BY.1-COL-1
75, 76, 77 Town of Colonie, New York
78 New York State Museum
80 Private collection
83 New York State Museum
84 (top) James M. Deem
(bottom left and right) New York State Museum
87 Library of Congress DIG-ppmsca-08979
88–89 Texas State Preservation Board
90 Bridgeman Art Library
93 (top) James M. Deem
(bottom) Courtesy of the Penn Museum, image # 199808, Morton Collection
94 Courtesy of the Penn Museum, Morton Collection
95 James M. Deem
96 James M. Deem
97 James M. Deem
98 Amanda Danning
99 Jeff Dunn
100–101 Private collection
103 Getty Images/Jerry Cooke
104, 105, 106 New York State Museum
108 Getty Images/Jerry Cooke
109, 110, 111, 112 New York State Museum
113 (top) New York State Museum
(bottom) James M. Deem
115 Parsons Child and Family Center, Albany, New York
116–17 James M. Deem
119 Library of Congress, DIG-ppmsca-11406
120, 121, 122 Bureau of Reclamation
123 (top) William A. Keleher Collection, Center for Southwest Research, University Libraries, University of New Mexico
(bottom) AP Images/Courtesy of Lisa Croft, U.S. Bureau of Reclamation
124 Library of Congress USZ62-98515
125 Bureau of Reclamation
126 (top left and right, bottom left) J. E. Brasher
(bottom right)
James M. Deem
127 James M. Deem
128 Bureau of Reclamation
129 Amanda Danning
130–31 James M. Deem
133 W. B. D. Gray Collection, Box 8, Folder 3, American Heritage Center, University of Wyoming
134 (top) Getty Images/Fotosearch
(bottom) Uinta County Museum, Evanston, Wyoming
135 James M. Deem
136 ((left) James M. Deem
(right) University of Wyoming Anthropology Department HRR Files
139 Library of Congress USZ62-96518
150 James M. Deem
151 (top) Reconstruction by Sharon A. Long; photograph by Chip Clark, National Museum of Natural History, Smithsonian Institution
(bottom) Frank Kelly

INDEX

Page numbers in *italics* refer to photos and their captions.